Chrysalis Reader

VOLUME 2

DAVID B. ELLER
PUBLISHER

JOHN L. HITCHCOCK
CHAIR, EDITORIAL BOARD

CAROL S. LAWSON
SERIES EDITOR

ALICE B. SKINNER
ART EDITOR

VOSS FINN
COVER ART

ROBERT LAWSON
SENIOR EDITOR

SUSANNA VAN RENSSELAER
ASSOCIATE EDITOR/LAYOUT DESIGN

PETER AND ELSA BETHANIS
FICTION EDITORS

SUSAN FLAGG POOLE
DEVELOPMENT EDITOR

CYNTHIA K.J. RICHARD
EDITORIAL ASSISTANT

JOEL FRIEDLANDER
BOOK DESIGN

Twelve Gates to the City

SPIRITUAL VIEWS ON THE JOURNEY FROM THIRTY AUTHORS

Edited by Carol S. Lawson

CHRYSALIS BOOKS

Imprint of the Swedenborg Foundation
West Chester, Pennsylvania

THE CHRYSALIS READER is a book series that examines themes related to the universal quest for wisdom. Inspired by the Swedenborg Foundation journal *Chrysalis,* each volume presents original short stories, essays, poetry, and art exploring the spiritual dimensions of a chosen theme. Works are selected by the series editor. For information on future themes or submission of original writings, contact Carol S. Lawson, Editor, Route 1, Box 184, Dillwyn, Virginia 23936.

Printed on recycled paper and bound in the United States of America

LIBRARY OF CONGRESS CATALOGING-IN-PUBLICATION DATA

Twelve gates to the city: spiritual views on the journey
from thirty authors / edited by Carol S. Lawson
p. cm. —(Chrysalis Reader: v. 2)
ISBN 0-87785-226-X
1. Spiritual life—Literary collections. 2. Swedenborg, Emanuel, 1688–1772
—Influence. 3. Mysticism—Literary collections. 4. American literature—20th century. I. Lawson, Carol S. II. Series.
PS509.S62T84 1996
810.8´0382—dc20 95-46639
CIP

CHRYSALIS BOOKS
Imprint of the Swedenborg Foundation
320 North Church Street
West Chester, Pennsylvania 19380

Contents

The Owl Shall Hoot at the Window

ALL GATES ARE OPENINGS into another place, time, and understanding. As we step into those new surroundings, we become witnesses and participants in the wonders, truths, and untruths that are there. Our eyes and past, like windows, filter and mold our experience. If we allow ourselves to listen, however, we momentarily leave our world to enter into a universe with shared myths, metaphors, and representations.

If an owl hoots at the window, presumably we are inside, enjoying the security of our home, our past. But outside at the window there is another world. Our attention is called by another form of life, an owl, speaking its own language. Two different worlds meet. What alien and dark meanings are there?

You also, O Ethiopians,
shall be killed by my sword
And he will stretch out his hand
against the north,
and destroy Assyria;
and he will make Nineveh a desolation
a dry waste like the desert.
Herds shall lie down in it,
every wild animal,
the desert owl and the
screech owl

shall lodge on its capitals;
the owl shall hoot at the window,
the raven croak on the threshold;
for its cedar work will be laid bare.

Is this the exultant city
that lived secure,
that said to itself
"I am, and there is no one else"?
What a desolation it has become,
a lair for wild animals!
Everyone who passes by it
hisses and shakes the fist.

—ZEPHANIAH 2:12-15

We see and hear a series of ominous signs. Nineveh, a beautiful city, will be a ruin in which wild animals will lie down. Owls will lodge in its capitals, the owl will hoot at the window, and the black raven will croak at the threshold. Why all this?

This appears to be a useless bit of history. What is Nineveh to us? Yet this passage has been read and studied in the world's most published book ever since it was written. Why? Because sacred language speaks to anyone who can understand it. It is like the myth of a people that is told repeatedly over the centuries. It is speaking of what is always true. Nineveh took pride in itself, as though it need consider no one else. As we become locked in our own worlds and feel we need not consider the rest of life, we too are in danger of being taken over by our own limitations. Applied to the world today, if we don't have regard for the whole of life and the welfare of our planet, we will lose what sustains us. Here in the guise of history we have sacred language. It is sacred because it is always true. It is true in all times and places and of use to anyone who cares to see its symbolism. That is why it is sacred.

The power of the sacred is that it is available for use by anyone; anyone can respond to the hoot of the owl at the window. It is a kind of open vessel which each can adapt to his or her own use, just as I applied Zephaniah to our world ecological situation. Of course this is not the only application. We each have different windows (and understandings) and owls.

The mystic Emanuel Swedenborg (1688–1772) came to a deep understanding of sacred language by an interesting way. Having literally mastered all of the science of his day (as reported in his 153 scientific publications), he then took on understanding God. He experimented with automatic writing, interpreted his own dreams, and tried a variety of ways to experience the divine but abandoned them.

Finally he came to a primitive solution. He would assume God was in the words of the Bible, and he would read it as though consulting a living God. Certain passages leapt out at him. These he wrote down in a private journal. The book looks like a dull collection of biblical passages until you realize these were the ones that were alive for him. He sought the owl at the window and was delighted to find it. The book ends with God writing through his hand. This was a beginning for him. In a few years the twelve volumes of his *Arcana Coelestia (Heavenly Secrets)* started to appear. They are rich with the wonders of the sacred language.

How varied the world is. Some people have windows and don't notice what is outside. Others enter through the gate and commune with the owl who represents wisdom. It is the kind of situation where it all depends on us. It can vary all the way from an unheard owl to communing with wisdom itself.

WILSON VAN DUSEN says he is the only aged mystic who rides a motorcycle. Wilson is a clinical psychologist, a student of Eastern and Western philosophies, and author of many books, including *Uses, The Presence of Other Worlds,* and *The Natural Depth in Man.*

PREFACE . CAROL S. LAWSON

The Spiral Path

> *Ariadne, the daughter of King Minos, fell in love with the handsome Theseus the moment she saw him disembark from the boat that had brought the pitiful group of Athenian youths and maidens [as sacrifice] for the Minotaur. . . . Ariadne turned for help, then, to the crafty Daedalus, by whose art the labyrinth had been constructed. Daedalus simply presented her with a skein of linen thread, which the visiting hero might fix to the entrance and unwind as he went into the maze. It is, indeed, very little that we need! But lacking that, the adventure into the labyrinth is without hope.*[1]
>
> —JOSEPH CAMPBELL

THIS BOOK HAS BEEN WRITTEN FOR, AND BY, today's hero with a thousand faces, people who are experiencing what it means to find and follow a "golden thread." And what *is* the slender thread that Joseph Campbell says is "all we need" to guide us? Perhaps the thread is simply the *imagination and willingness* to undertake the journey. Perhaps the thread is the tungsten alloy of living out our own truths. And where are we being led by the golden thread on its spiral path? John Hitchcock suggests that "our search for experience of the divine, for aliveness, for something felt as acceptance by something greater than ourselves" has taken humanity on an inner journey. "The way is labyrinthine in its very essence."[2]

How difficult is it to find the inner meaning of life or to undertake the journey toward experiencing the divine? In this volume of the Chrysalis Reader, Alice Skinner points out that one way to get

---

1 Joseph Campbell. *The Hero with a Thousand Faces.* 2d ed. Princeton University Press, 1973.

2 John L. Hitchcock. *The New Labyrinth: A Journey of the Self.* Rockport, Massachusetts: John L. Hitchcock, 1994. p 1.

started is to look for gates. Walter Christie describes the predicament the modern hero faces in the midst of environmental chaos. Other writers voice the difficulties of getting started on the journey because of contemporary fears and hazards. Then Mary Kay McKeon Klein tells the story of the medieval hero Hildegard, a model of hope, who lived almost a thousand years ago. This story is followed by a cross-section of many views from writers, poets, and artists—people on spiral paths following the golden thread. These reporters use amazing imagery to describe the rotaries and roundabouts that open to new thought and deeper consciousness. The last essay by Ralph Pray gives us a surprise insight from the top of Mt. Fuji.

At the inception of this Reader, its theme was "windows," but as the essays began to weave together, the new theme of "gates" emerged. Windows are openings that show us the possibilities, and gates are how we move into the promise of new realities. As the speaker indicates in Robert Bly's poem "He Wanted to Live His Life Over," he is encouraged to open the door, walk down to the river, and "pretend this boat is my life."

We would like to think that the Swedish mystic, Emanuel Swedenborg—who used his scientific orientation to explore the world of spirit and and who emphasized a life of usefulness as a spiritual journey—would be pleased with the vistas opened by this volume. For one of his insights is that there *are* innumerable gates and many paths toward them.

Robin Larsen. *Spiral Labyrinth.* Design from the floor of the nave Chartres Cathedral, France, twelfth century. "The point or centre, in those labyrinths depicted in the pavement floors of many medieval cathedrals, is sometimes (as it originally was at Chartres) a depiction of Theseus and the Minotaur. The symbolism is that of the 'original' Cretan labyrinth—an initiatory hero test, the overcoming of death at the centre, and a subsequent return or rebirth into life, a regeneration on a higher winding . . . treading the maze was a pilgrimage to Jerusalem in miniature."—Jill Purse. *The Mystic Spiral.* Art and Cosmos Series. London: Thames and Hudson, Ltd., 1974. p. 29.

CAROL S. LAWSON, Chrysalis Reader's editor, is also the executive editor of *Birding*, journal of the American Birding Association, and a former director of the hazardous waste information program of the U.S. Environmental Protection Agency.

Twelve Gates to the City

SPIRITUAL VIEWS ON THE JOURNEY
FROM THIRTY AUTHORS

Looking for a Gate

I give you the end of a golden string,
Only wind it into a ball:
It will lead you in at heaven's gate,
Built in Jerusalem's wall.[1]

IF THE WAY TO HEAVEN is difficult, how can a golden string lead us to the pearly gates?

> Some people believe it is hard to live the life that leads to heaven, because they have heard that you have to renounce the world and give up the desires people associate with the body and the flesh, and "live spiritually." But people who renounce the world and live by the spirit in this way acquire a mournful life, one that is not receptive of heavenly joy. Rather, in order to be receptive of heaven's life, people should by all means live in the world and be involved in its duties and business. In this way, through a moral and civic life, we engender a spiritual life. There is no other way spiritual life can take shape in us, no other way our spirits can be prepared for heaven.[2]

Opposite:
William Blake.
Los Entering the Grave.
Relief etching with pen, watercolor, and gold, 6¼×8⅝ inches, ca. 1804. Yale Center for British Art, Paul Mellon Collection.

[1] Blake, William. *Jerusalem,* plate 77. In *The Complete Poems.* Harmondsworth, Middlesex, England: Penguin Classics, 1977. p. 797.

[2] Adapted from Emanuel Swedenborg. *Heaven and Hell,* paragraph no. 528. In George Dole, *A View from Within.* New York: Swedenborg Foundation, 1985. p. 81. Swedenborg numbered the paragraphs in his works. In Swedenborgian studies it is customary to reference a particular text by the book's title and Swedenborg's paragraph number, as the numbers are uniform in all editions.

THE STRING BECOMES GOLDEN as a result of dedicated action . . .

Until one is committed, there is hesitancy, the chance to draw back, always ineffectiveness . . . the moment one definitely commits oneself, then providence moves too. All sorts of things occur to help one that would never otherwise have occurred . . .

Whatever you can do,
or dream you can, begin it.
Boldness has genius,
power and magic in it.[3]

West Door of Cathedral. Nova Scotian monel metal, hand-wrought, twentieth century. Bryn Athyn, Pennsylvania. Photograph by Michael Pitcairn.

DEVOTION TO THE DIVINE is at the center of the ball.

In my understanding
I saw God
in a point.

In seeing this
I saw God is in all things.

God works in creatures because
God is in the mid-point of everything
and does all that is done.[4]

[3] Johann Wolfgang von Goethe. "Until One is Committed." In Robert Bly, James Hillman, and Michael Meade. *The Rag and Bone Shop of the Heart.* New York: Harper Collins Publishers, 1993. p. 235.

[4] Brendan Doyle. *Meditations with Julian of Norwich.* Santa Fe: Bear & Co., 1983. p. 37.

WE HOLD FAST to the golden string in hard times . . .

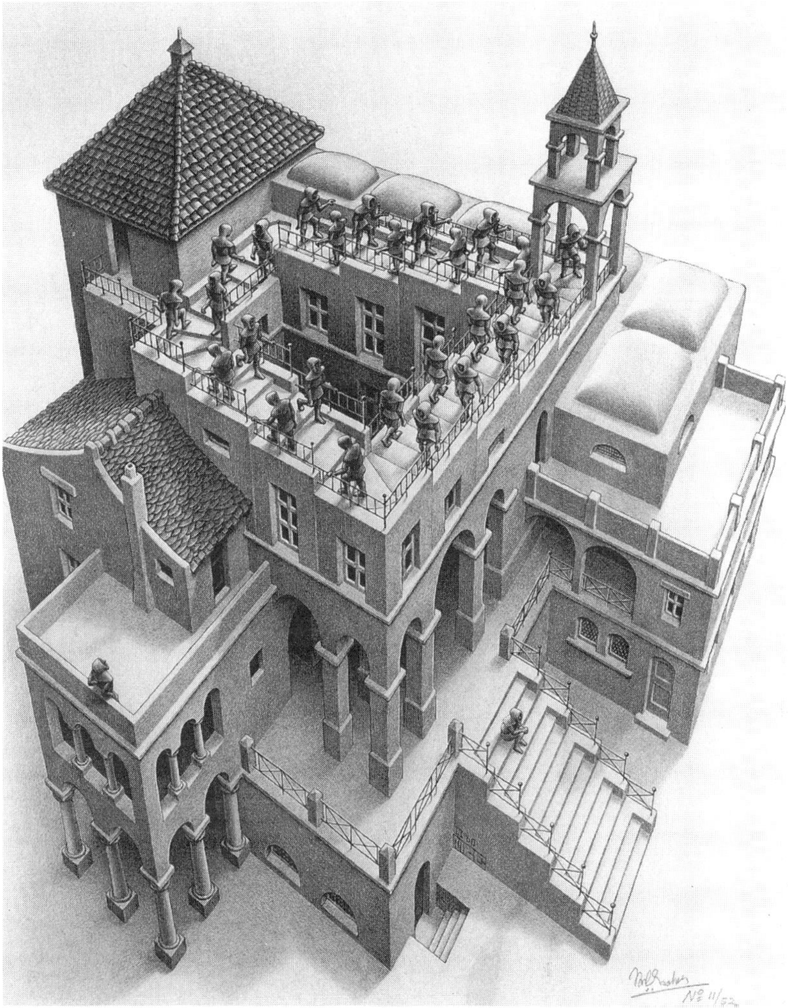

M.C. Escher. *Ascending and Descending.* Lithograph, 1960. Baarn, Holland: Cordon Art B.V., 1995.

Well, son, I'll tell you;
Life for me ain't been
  no crystal stair.
It's had tacks in it,
And splinters,
And boards torn up,
And places with no
  carpet on the floor—
Bare.
But all the time
I'se been a-climbin' on,
And reachin' landin's,
And turnin' corners,
And sometimes goin' in the dark
Where there ain't been no light.
So boy, don't you turn back.
Don't you set down on the steps
'Cause you finds it's kinder hard.
Don't you fall now—
For I'se still goin', honey,
I'se still climbin'.
And life for me ain't been no crystal stair.[5]

---

[5] Langston Hughes. "Mother to Son." In E. Ethelbert Miller, *In Search of Color Everywhere: A Collection of African–American Poetry.* New York: Stewart, Tabori & Chang, 1994. p. 69.

AND SOMETIMES STUMBLE BACKWARDS over the cord.

I fled Him, down the nights and down the days;
  I fled Him, down the arches of the years;
I fled Him, down the labyrinthine ways
  Of my own mind; and in the mist of tears
I hid from Him, and under running laughter . . .
Across the margent of the world I fled,
  And troubled the gold gateways of the stars,
  Smited for shelter on their clangèd bars.[6]

Hugo Sperger. *Sorrow and Hope.* Oil on masonite, 1983. Morehead, Kentucky: Folk Art Collection at Morehead State University.

BUT THE GOLDEN THREAD LEADS upward to discovery.

Pain can make a whole winter bright,
Like fever, force us to live deep and hard,
Betrayal focus in a peculiar light
All we have ever dreamed or known or heard,
And from great shocks we do recover.
Like Wright's hotel we have been fashioned
To take earthquake and stand upright still.
Alive among the wreckage, we discover
Death or ruin is not less impassioned
Than we ourselves, and not less terrible,
Since we nicely absorb and can use them all.[7]

[6] Francis Thompson. "The Hound of Heaven." In Louis Untermeyer. *Modern British Poetry.* New York: Harcourt, Brace & Co., 1942. p. 97.

[7] May Sarton. "Humpty Dumpty." In *Collected Poems.* New York: W.W. Norton & Co., Inc., 1974. p. 149.

AND LEADS US to wisdom.

Here is the test of wisdom
Wisdom is not finally tested
in schools,
Wisdom cannot be pass'd
from one having it to
another not having it,
Wisdom is of the soul,
is not susceptible of proof,
is its own proof,
Applies to all stages and objects
and qualities and is content,
Is the certainty of the reality
and immortality of things,
and the excellence of things;
Something there is in the float
of the sight of things
that provokes it out of the
soul.[8]

1890 Gate to Harvard Yard, Cambridge, Massachusetts.
The inscription on the lintel reads, "Enter to Grow in Wisdom."

AND SUSTAINS US with goodness.

Good has no fear;
Good is itself, whatever comes.
It grows, and makes, and bravely
Persuades, beyond all tilt of wrong;
Stronger than anger, wiser than strategy,
Enough to subdue cities and men
If we believe it with a long courage of truth . . .
Thank God our time is now when wrong
Comes up to face us everywhere,
Never to leave us till we take
The longest stride of soul men ever took.
Affairs are now soul size.[9]

---

8 Walt Whitman. "Song of the Open Road." In *Leaves of Grass.* New York: Doubleday, Doran & Co., 1940. pp. 6–7.

9 Christopher Fry. *A Sleep of Prisoners.* New York & London: Oxford University Press, 1951. p. 47.

UNTIL WE ENVISION THE GATES **at journey's end.**

When each day
is sacred

when each hour
is sacred

when each instant
is sacred

earth and you
space and you
bearing the sacred
through time

you'll reach
the fields of light.[10]

ALICE SKINNER, a psychologist and the president of the Swedenborg Foundation, looks for gateways on her travels from her home on the coast of Maine.

Katsushika Hokusai. *Under Mannen Bridge at Fukagawa.* In the series *Thirty-six Views of Fuji.* Polychrome, woodblock print, $15\frac{3}{16} \times 10\frac{1}{8}$ inches, nineteenth century. New York: Metropolitan Museum of Art, Rogers Fund, 1922 (JP 1332).

---

[10] Guillevic. *The Task.* In Phil Cousineau. *The Soul of the World: A Modern Book of Hours.* San Francisco: Harper, 1993.

PART I

In the Shadow of the Mountain

WALTER R. CHRISTIE

Transcending Destruction

AT THE END OF THE PETROLEUM AGE as we widen the ozone hole and slash to the ground the life-giving rain forests, I'm bewildered at my joy in being alive. Despite the global extinction that threatens life on Earth as we know it, I live in constant relationship with great natural beauty and carry within my soul deep conviction of divine mystery. In the darkness of the clash between our materialistic culture and the environment, is participation in beauty and mystery just denial or mere naiveté?

Andrew Harvey, a contemporary mystic, writes:

> We are certainly at the end of a civilization, a whole cycle of history, and, possibly, at the end of the world. The facts of our global crisis—a crisis that is at once political and economic, psychological and environmental—show us clearly that the human race has no hope of survival unless it chooses to undergo a total change of heart, a massive, quite unprecedented spiritual transformation. . . . Many experts agree that we have, at the most fifteen or twenty years left before extreme crisis becomes unalterable catastrophe. Tielhard de Chardin wrote, "Humankind is being taken to the point where it will have to decide between suicide and adoration."[1]

Opposite:
Voss Finn
Transcending Destruction.
Watercolor, 1995.
Cincinnati.

These forthright and prophetic words grab us by the collar and pull us eye to eye with the urgency of our future. But unfortunately our surge of spiritual adrenaline is brief; massive efforts by extraordinary people have not been able to turn our collective will from

[1] Andrew Harvey and Mark Matousek. *Dialogues with a Modern Mystic.* Wheaton, Illinois: Theosophical Publishing House, 1994. p. 27.

practices of unremitting material voraciousness and cruelty toward ourselves and other life forms.

In our desperation we need teachers, great individuals who can help us bear the tension between the harsh facts of planetary destruction and our deepest dreams for a creative, harmonious world. We need inspiring visionaries who have experienced the truth that beauty leads to mystery, and mystical awareness points to relationship with a larger reality that might save us from the destructiveness of our too small, secular selves.

Of course, we could choose to drop out and enjoy the fading beauty of Earth's final years. In this way we might avoid suffering the pain of realizing our lack of restraint. But escape is not an option. Inseparable from each other and conscious, we really have no choice but to acknowledge that our age is not one of peace, but instead one of multiple religious wars, massive atrocities, global epidemics, and moral challenges beyond imagination. The sickening of the atmosphere, water, vegetation, and creatures of our great planet is all too apparent. Instead of seeking a lost Eden we would do better to meet the challenge of comprehending the totality of our species' destructive power while we cultivate, through appreciation of beauty and revelation of oneness, our inner capacity to transcend such destructiveness and live in harmony with the Earth.

Naming the Darkness

A first step toward that goal would be to answer these questions: (1) Where shall we look to understand the totality of human darkness? (2) How can we hold the opposites until we are transformed ? (3) Who can teach us about the beauty and mystery of the light?

A simple source of information on our species' darkness is found in the daily newspapers, but this morass of uncritically processed facts is merely an information glut and takes us nowhere unless joined with inner correlates within the human heart. In *Owning Your Own Shadow,* Robert Johnson instructs us on methods of identifying disowned elements of both inner and outer realities, and he offers us a method of holding the warring opposites until a force (the divine) speaks through the psyche and lifts our worldly identity from the field of conflicting dualities to the transcendent unity of divine paradox.

Johnson takes us into a region of the heart, haunted by unowned instincts and denied spiritual aspirations. In this darkness, he tells us, lies a depth of psychic reality we rarely plumb unless we are totally helpless. With our backs to the wall we may find the ground of spiritual experience, the place when the "unstoppable bullet hits the impenetrable wall."[2] Here raw, numinous energy transforms earthly conflict into divine paradox.

We will go to almost any length to avoid this painful paradox; but in that refusal we only confine ourselves to the useless experience of contradiction. Contradiction brings the crushing burden of meaninglessness. One can endure any suffering if it has meaning: but meaninglessness is unbearable. Contradiction is barren and destructive, yet paradox is creative. It is a powerful embracing of reality . . . paradox makes room for grace and mystery.[3]

Johnson's model for holding opposites is the mandorla. The word *mandorla* (Italian) actually refers to the almond shaped ellipse formed by the intersection of two circles (above). This ancient figure, originally a representation of the Goddess and her consort and later of Mary and Christ, is also a schema of the anatomy and physiology of the spiritual heart. One circle holds all of our darkest impulses, deeds, and tragedies, while the other contains our highest aspirations, ideals, and dreams. As tension builds between the polarities, the empty space between the circles lies waiting. The mandorla is a space of revelation, ready to be filled with insights about new possibilities for ensouled personal and planetary life.

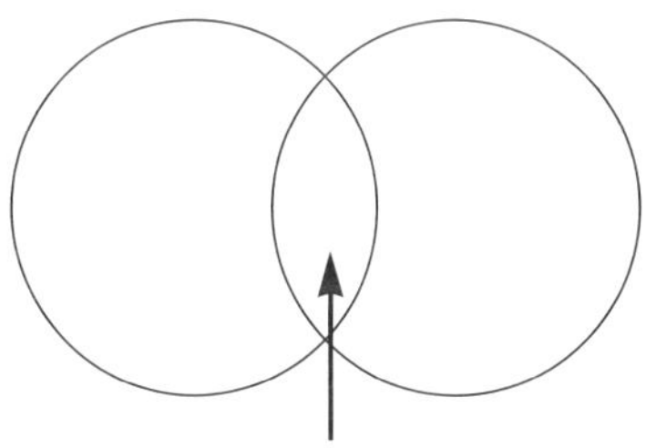

mandorla

Filling the Circles

Taking this inventory, we must look deep into the heart of our economy and see our great attachment to material culture and the growth-crazed international power structure that supports it, and then with painful honesty we must stir our own shameful business into the dark negative circle of the mandorla.

> Having constructed our mandorla, we begin the painful task of filling the dark circle with all we know of Earth's deteriorating conditions. With our understanding of the consequences of a projected 9 billion people by the year 2025 we pour into the darkness the vision of a toxic environment, the extinction of thousands of species, the hectic growth of megacities with ac-

---

[2] Robert Johnson. *Owning Your Own Shadow.* San Francisco: Harper, 1993. p. 92.
[3] Ibid., p. 74.

companying deforestation, groundwater depletion, soil erosion, spread of epidemic disease, and large-scale malnutrition. Envisioning these overpopulated, unstable regions, we acknowledge what we know about our collective behavior, namely that war, genocide, and repression of the poor will increase beyond any hope of sustainable life for future generations.

Then having taken our global inventory, we turn our penetrating vision to our personal lives. Then, with humility, we add our own shameful business to the darkness.[4]

Teachers

The weight of the dark circle almost crushes our hearts. Who then can teach us about the light? As we look around, no ecological savior steps forth, and no government or organization offers a clear, effective rallying point for an environmentally sound, humane world order. In this vacuum, perhaps our souls may choose teachers.

In this spirit I chose Hildegard of Bingen, Meister Eckhart, John Keats, Ralph Waldo Emerson, and Rachael Carson. In my own view, these great individuals loved the beauty of the natural world, lived deep in the mystery of life, yet also knew the full darkness of the human heart. The teachers saw within the heart a greater light that unites us all.

Hildegard of Bingen (1098–1179)

Hildegard von Bingen was an enormously talented Rhineland abbess with skills in medicine, writing, and music. She experienced in mid-life, in the midst of a protracted physical illness, a mystical breakthrough that led her to envision the spirit that flowed through all life as *viriditas*—holy greenness.[5] She said:

> There is no creation that does not have a radiance. Be it greenness or seed, blossom or beauty, it could not be creation without it . . . the word is living, being, spirit, all verdant greening, all creativity.[6]

In a later essay in this book, you will read a fuller account of Hildegard's visions of the City of God, which was her way to reimage this world and to teach others to do the same.

---

[4] Timothy Weiskel. "Some Notes from Belshaz'zar's Feast." Keynote speech, conference on "God, the Environment and the Good Life." University of Hampshire, Nov. 11–13, 1993. pp. 6–16.

[5] Matthew Fox, ed. *The Illuminations of Hildegard of Bingen.* Santa Fe: Bear & Co., 1985. p. 30.

[6] Ibid., p. 18.

Meister Eckhart (1260–1328)

Meister Eckhart's time had much in common with our own. A population explosion was followed by a sudden mini ice age and floods with crop failures, widespread famine, and a growing separation between the rich and the poor. Authorities could do little to help, for corruption in high places was common, and with it lawlessness, the decline of knighthood and degeneration of the chivalric tradition, and an increased gap between real and ideal. Greed ruled the church which battled constantly with chaotic secular governments for money and territory.[7]

Radical movements like those of Beguines, witches, and mystical sects rose to meet this corruption, disorder, and social injustice, but these groups could hardly assuage the spirit of despair, guilt, and "end of times" that led many women to wonder about bringing children into the world.[8]

Eckhart, a Rhineland mystic like Hildegard, was an accomplished abbot and theological teacher. Influenced by his Celtic familial roots and his affinity with the laywomen's movement, he reached for mystical understanding of the reality of God's relationship to the individual soul. He found immediate, intimate, reciprocal connections between the depths of the human psyche and the creative force of the universe, and he laid out four mystical ways—the affirmation of images, the negation of images, the creative path, and the transformative path. Often seen as a figure capable of integrating Eastern and Western philosophies, he is perhaps the Christian West's most formidable teacher of mystical revelation. Nature was his teacher, and the Divine Feminine was omnipresent in his thinking and writing. More than many other Western mystics he could speak from both the emptiness and the creative fullness of the divine.[9] Eckhart wrote:

> God is a great underground river that no one can dam up and no one can stop.[10]

He also said:

> I once had a dream.
> I dreamt that I, even though a man, was pregnant,
> pregnant, and full with Nothingness like a woman who
> is with child. And that out of this Nothingness God was
> born.[11]

---

[7] Matthew Fox. *Breakthrough: Meister Eckhart's Creation Spirituality in New Translation.* New York: Doubleday, 1991. pp.10–18.
[8] Ibid., pp. 10–18.
[9] Ibid., pp. 43–48.
[10] Matthew Fox. *Meditations with Meister Eckhart.* Santa Fe: Bear & Co., 1983. p. 16.
[11] Ibid., p. 71.

Eckhart told us that:

> God's darkness
> is superessential darkness.
> A mystery behind mystery,
> a mystery within mystery that no light has ever penetrated.[12]

John Keats (1795–1821)

In his brief twenty-six years of life Keats left us 150 poems and a series of brilliant letters that examine the spiritual and metaphysical dynamics of the creative process. Keats found in nature the sensuous experiences that awaken imagination, the faculty that could discern beauty and truth. His way of the heart was one of suffering and love, but all in the embrace of a creativity that transcended death. Through his poetry and letters he reveals for us the power of imagination as a spiritual faculty and imagination's linkage with all of nature. Keats said:

> [T]he excellence of every art is its intensity, capable of making all disagreeables evaporate, from their being in close relationship with beauty and truth.[13]

He said:

> Call the world if you please "The vale of Soul-making."[14]

For Keats, imagination, the chief faculty of poetry, was the "desire for reality transfigured into a more perfect image of the real."[15] Contacting the real is thus fundamentally a religious act, and the key to achieving this contact lies in the liberated flow of poetic imagination, energized by the superabundant outflow of life's mystery. Mystery "frees humanity from the world of circumstance and from the wornout frame of self-centeredness."[16] Thus allegorical living is not a fantasy to avoid harsh reality, but a romance or spiritual adventure that encounters the real. This romance, the poet's greatest action in time, is the path to both enter and redeem the world.[17]

Ralph Waldo Emerson (1803–1882)

Emerson was a lecturer, essayist, and poet. He was a champion of American values of self-reliance and self-definition, but working within the greater context of the unity of all being. The central intellect of the American Transcendental movement, Emerson raised public consciousness of the divinity of nature and proclaimed nature to be our true teacher and classroom. His way, like many Eastern

[12] Ibid., p. 43.
[13] Andre Rodriguez. *Book of the Heart.* Hudson, New York: Lindesfarne Press, 1993. p. 39.
[14] Ibid., p. 117.
[15] Ibid., p. 11.
[16] Ibid., p. 12.
[17] Ibid., p. 13.

paths, was through the mind, but a mind grounded in natural order. In many ways we have not gone beyond him, and his fallen standard lies waiting to be lifted by the next champion of the self. He said:

> There is a soul at the center of nature and over the will of every man, so that no one of us can harm the universe. It has so infused its strong attachment into nature that we prosper when we accept its advice, and when we struggle to wound its creatures our hands are glued to our sides, or they beat their own breasts. The whole course of things goes to teach us faith. We need only obey. There is guidance for each of us, and by lowly listening we shall hear the right word.[18]

Emerson said that:

> In the woods, we return to reason and faith. There I feel nothing can befall me in life,—no disgrace, no calamity, (leaving me my eyes,) which nature cannot repair. Standing on the bare ground,—my head bathed by the blithe air, and uplifted into infinite space,—all mean egotism vanishes. I become a transparent eyeball. I am nothing. I see all. The currents of the Universal Being circulate through me; I am part and particle of God.[19]

Rachel Carson (1907–1964)

Rachel Carson, in a most selfless way, integrated ecological science and spiritual understanding with such deftness of skill and seamless unity that we hardly realize we are in the presence of a mystic. In the midst of a demanding life and facing her own imminent death from cancer, she wrote *Silent Spring*, a book that changed the world. She is an admirable example of an integrated modern person who was open to the mystery of life and yet skilled in the discipline of science and the craft of writing. The recently published letters between Rachel and her friend Dorothy reveal that she was an ecstatic nature mystic of the highest order. She said:

> Contemplating the teeming life of the shore, we have an uneasy sense of the communication of some universal truth that lies just beyond our grasp. What is the message signaled by the hordes of diatoms, flashing their microscopic lights in the night sea? What truth is expressed by the legions of the barnacles, whitening the rocks with their habitations, each small creature within finding the necessities of its existence in the sweep of the surf? And what is the meaning of so tiny a being as the transparent wisp of protoplasm that is a sea lace, existing for some reason inscrutable to us—a reason that demands its presence by the trillion amid the

[18] Ralph Waldo Emerson. *Emerson's Essays, First and Second Series.* New York: Harper & Row, 1951. p. 99.

[19] Ralph Waldo Emerson. *Nature and Other Writings.* Boston: Shambhala, 1994. pp. 7–8.

rocks and weeds of the shore? The meaning haunts and ever eludes us, and in its very pursuit we approach the ultimate mystery of life itself.[20]

Conclusion

Gathering five mystical friends to help me face the darkness of our world crisis, I prepared myself for a gift from each. Hildegard, with a healing creativity that arises from the darkness of her physical pain, offers the vision of "viriditas," holy greenness flowing through all that is, the vegetative Goddess ever renewing our world. Eckhart, brilliant and versatile, shows both men and women how to be pregnant with God, to be empty and dark, and then to be filled with a spirit and light that restores the unity of all being. Youthful Keats, lover of beauty, master of poesies and transformational imagination, offers us a path of creative suffering that opens the heart to a love beyond understanding—a love that binds all beings in a web of meaning and mystery. Emerson seizes our resilience and, turning us both toward nature and the East, he reveals within our minds a spark of divinity that awakens us to our true identity. Finally, Rachel Carson, writing about processes of nature, unites scientific observation and spiritual devotion as she leads us to the unseen mystery at the edge of the sea of our being.

The gifts of the five luminaries are extraordinary. They encourage us to treat what arises within our own hearts as pure gold. In this spirit let us pour into the light circle of the mandorla our brightest dreams, best sunsets, favorite places, most loved creatures. Then actively remembering all that has quickened our imaginations and enlivened our beings from childhood to the present, let us bring into the circle all whom we love.

Listening and Waiting

To know when mystery moves in the mandorla space is no easy task. Sometimes it presents imperatives—Clean up the local dump! Give money to Tibetan refugees! Often, however, activity within the mandorla space is more subtle, and the messages do not fit the culture's categories of action. For achievement-oriented persons, urgings of the self may seem passive, otherworldly, or at times infuriating. Plant flowers on your mother's grave, the mandorla says. Read an hour of good literature a day, it adds, leaving us bewildered by the relationship between such acts and the City of God.

The key to mandorla work—in fact to all deep inner work—is trust and surrender. There is a center of knowing in us concerned not only with our own well-being, but with the health and harmony of all that surrounds us. You have a soul, this center quietly teaches us.

---

[20] Paul Brooks. *The House of Life.* Boston: Houghton Mifflin Co., 1989. p. 328.

Planetary life has a soul, it continues, and your soul is part of it. Trust the messages, it says, no matter how strange and seemingly irrelevant. Such trust is an act of faith, devotion, and readiness.

Thus, holding in our hearts the two circles of the mandorla we begin the active waiting by watching the world without and the empty space within for traces of fascinations, synchronous events, painful circumstances that touch our hearts, sudden intuitions, dreams, revelations, and body symptoms that urge us toward action. The messages that appear as we wait sometimes may come with sadness and nostalgia, and such moods may cause us to miss the gift of love hidden in the experience of loss. Other times, however, mandorla messages rush in with great joy, wiping out skeins of self-defeating thoughts that straggle across the inner sky of our minds.

Messages are not the only valuable aspect of this work. The mandorla also teaches us how to wait, how to sit with our luminary friends until an awareness greater than our own speaks. The real mystery of mandorla work lies in this open waiting. Waiting can seem like a resignation to death itself, yet waiting can be the highest action of all.

This is not to say that environmental actions like saving wetlands and recycling are not critical and should be discontinued, but more to point out that these actions in themselves have not changed our species' fundamental race toward ecological destruction. In the spirit of the wisdom of waiting, thus our mystic friends remind us that to save the world we must first save ourselves, for only an inner center knows our true identity and right relationship with this beautiful and mysterious planet that is our home.

This is our position at the end of the petroleum age as we try a last-ditch effort to exploit Earth's diminishing resources, pump up the global economy, and make our materialistic dream come true. Rich or poor, by virtue of being members of the human community, we are all deep in this darkness. In our helplessness, however, we may choose to follow the practice of the mandorla. In that practice we agree to look straight in the eye of the nightmare we are creating, while simultaneously listening to the teachers, who come to us willingly, despite the ominousness of the times and our own uncertain commitment to change. These five mystics, and many others readers may choose, step into our hearts and wait with us until grace visits with revelation. Perhaps revelation will come quickly, and we will know in time how we must be and what we must do to enter the city of the divine.

WALTER R. CHRISTIE is a certified psychiatrist and Fellow of the American Psychiatric Association. He is currently director of Psychiatric Outpatient Services at the Maine Medical Center. He is a founder of the C.G. Jung Center of Brunswick, Maine. He also has a master's degree in the Fine Arts with a writing specialty from Vermont College and lives in Freeport, Maine, with his wife, two dogs, and a cat.

PETER LAYTON

Licked Life

like a little
blood of the vine
two years Napa County
pick the plump bellies
always touched same's
abdomens black
widow spider
half drunk at work half
or whole
crazed on the orchard sun
up there blames me
failed my daughters failed
my failed marriage
Janet curses me again
but's the boss
Mr. Genoa face
blown up pincushioned color the
wooden-legged purple bleeders
coughed in busted
Spanish Italian English
why my baskets not ever filled
contemplate this detail
as each foot pad beats
the road
Highway 19 constant
pickers needed
wine summer

BARBARA SCHNEIDER

The Day They Bombed Bayreuth

Autumn Helen Lee

THE EARTH SMELLED FRESH, dark forest-earth. She lay on her stomach, her hands covering her ears, her body and face covering the ground. To the right her brother, the oldest. To her left, her younger brother. On the earth, in the earth. Tree stumps all around them. Her hands could not shield her ears from the noise. The airplanes were right above them. The sound of thousands of airplanes. She knew the sound: dive-bombers. But never before had they been that close.

Not one move. I must not make a single move, the airplanes see everything. When they suddenly dive, they can see even a squirrel. And then I will die. My brothers will die. Are my brothers alive?

She wanted to move her head but dared not do it. She took her hands off her ears, slowly, such a careful move, the airplanes would not be able to see it; she needed her ears to help her eyes. Then she tilted her head, three very small tilts, halts in-between, held her breath, now moving her eyes, not her head, towards the left. Then she saw him, her younger brother. He lay on the ground, wood-chips in his hair, motionless. Such panic. A terrible silent panic within her. Was he dead? She could not see his face. Why did he not move at all? Had he stopped breathing?

My brother has stopped breathing, my brother is dead. She stared at his back. Her heart, her lungs, each muscle in her body distilled into a single effort: finding a sign of life on her brother's back. Then she saw or thought she saw his shoulder move. So slightly, so very barely. Or was she mistaken? She needed proof. She waited, not breathing herself, for a sign of his breathing, a stir, anything. He was alive. Her younger brother was not dead.

She did not whisper a word, did not move her arm to touch his hair, but moved her head, carefully, then her eyes, back to the earth on which she lay. And felt such inexpressible relief.

A few moments later she dared move her head to the right and met her older brother's eyes; wide awake, no earth on his glasses, looking at her. And she knew those eyes had been fixed on her and her younger brother all the time, from the moment they threw themselves to the ground.

That overwhelming sound, unstoppable succession of sounds, ear-shattering, life-threatening, above them, that violent acceleration of power, planes diving, then the explosions, so very near. The longer she had to listen to the fury above her, the harder it became to keep on breathing. The fear that her heart would stop. Such terror. But no flames yet. No flames yet in her part of the forest.

Where was their mother? Would she ever see her again? In her black coat, with the red scarf. Where in that city they did not know was her mother, pushing the baby in the stroller? This morning when they parted, such a sunny day—the sun still shining on her back now—her mother had said, "I'll go and try to buy train tickets. Go back to the forest, it's the safest place. I'll meet you there as soon as I get some bread and the tickets. You'll have to wait, however long it'll take, by the stand of tall trees, near the rock, close to the path."

Then her mother had looked to the oldest. He, his eyes behind the glasses, did not nod or, if he did, only she had seen it. Then she kissed them and said, "At the sound of airplanes you must throw yourselves to the ground—immediately! Not run around, look for a better place, hesitate. You must act quickly—very, very quickly!" Again, she had looked to the oldest, then to her, the girl, and she, the girl, had nodded. Then her mother had tied her scarf in a hurry, hesitated before making the knot, and quickly kissed them again.

They had found the way to the forest easily. They had been there the day before, all five of them, on their way to their aunt—Aunt Lotte from Bayreuth who lived all by herself. But her apartment was crowded with relatives from other cities, fleeing the Russians as they were.

They had spent the night in Aunt Lotte's chicken coop. No chickens there; they had been eaten or sold or had run away. This morning her mother did not want them to stay in the chicken coop while she walked back to town. None of the children wanted to stay there, either. The stench was sickening.

When they arrived at the stand of tall trees, they saw, nearby, a clearing in the forest, a place full of stumps and cut-down trees. And because it was a fine, sunny day, and because they loved the smell of cut-down trees, and because things came to mind, games they could play, they went to the clearing and passed the time sliding alongside felled trees, climbing over them, see-sawing, catching each other and—best of all—balancing on the skinny ones. They had forgotten all about their mother's words and the war.

Then—it was in the middle of her balancing on the skinniest tree around—she could not remember what came first, the terrible sound or the terrible sight. From one moment to the next, they could not hear each other's voices, and when she looked up, the sky had disappeared. She wanted to run, run away from the planes, away from the stumps, towards the trees, the tall, tall trees, but her mother's words, in that very same instant, her urgent words "act quickly—very, very quickly", came back, stopping her, yet her body needed to escape, run like mad, disobey her mother's words, running away is wiser than staying here, run as fast as you can, away from the clearing, away from the sky, no, don't, don't, don't look for a better place. She could not save her brothers, she could not save herself, her feet nailed to the ground, she stood, unable to lift a leg, frozen, in the clearing. When he screamed, her older brother, already on the ground, screamed, so unlike him, "GET DOWN!!"
And she hit the earth with her body, her legs not bending, her face in a fever, her chest and arms a thump on the ground.

Then, for a long while, she felt nothing at all.

SHE DID NOT KNOW how much time had passed. The planes had left. The sun was still there, further away. Slowly, not quickly, they got up, shook the earth off their clothes, the wood chips, pine needles from their faces and each other's hair, looking. Looking for their mother. For the stroller. And then the younger brother pointed to something in the distance, something he saw on the forest path. "No, not there! There! Look! Don't you see? *There!*" His left arm, his hand, his forefinger stretched in the pointing, he ran from the spot next to his sister to another spot, now using both arms, hands and fingers, pointing, insisting, overcoming the distance. He said what he had seen was now around a bend on the forest path.

And they, all three of them, started to run. Down to the path, towards what the younger brother had seen in the distance. And now they could see what he had seen, a human shape, running, too. Running towards them. Something red, and something in the arms. Their running grew faster, knew no exhaustion, no stumbling, no hunger, no fear of bombs, it was her, the baby in her arms, the stroller not there, somewhere, running towards the running children, now without the scarf, red on the forest path, the children running, their arms stretched out towards the running mother, no stopping, no memory, no thought, and as they kept running towards her arms, towards the baby, before they had arrived, there came from their mother's mouth, her throat, the bottom of her womb, a shriek.

"THOMASKATRINJOHANNES THOMASKATRINJOHANNES To . . Ka . . . Jo . . ."

Then it stopped.

Arms holding each other. The baby in everyone's face. Noses pressed. Kisses on coats, on fingers. Sighs. One human clump holding everything. Life holding itself. Happiness. Absolute. She, Katrin—Katrin again. Whole. And immortal.

BARBARA SCHNEIDER writes and teaches fiction in New York City. She is also a playwright with a New York State Council on Arts fellowship, and has the Susan Smith Blackburn prize among her credits. Her plays have been presented at the O'Neill National Playwrights Conference, the Actors Theatre in Louisville, Philadelphia, Dallas, and New York City. She is also a Teaching Artist with the Young Playwrights Festival in New York. HELEN LEE is a Swedenborgian artist who lives in Pittsburgh and summers in Vermont.

BARBARA WILBUR

This Photograph

THE WORLD OF THIS PHOTOGRAPH must be dealt with in a straightforward pen-and-ink fashion. Hold the emotion of color at bay. Tell the story.

My story is about an event that took place fifteen days ago. It represents a yearly or twice-yearly event in my life. It is an event that every woman, hopefully, participates in or will participate in, in the future.

A mammogram is a diagnostic tool used to identify breast cancer. The picture that follows is of my right breast.

The event that I share took place at University of California Medical Center. It was my annual checkup.

The appointment was for 8:15 in the morning, everyone is fresh then, bright and alert. I have learned who the best technician is and my appointment was with her. I also had made sure that Dr. Sickles would be the reading radiologist, he is "The Man." I left the house early, planning my path: which lane to be in, which off-ramp to take, and exactly where I would park. *Upon arrival, I carefully placed the parking ticket on the dash, locked the car, and concentrated on putting the key in my purse in a pocket I would remember.* Then I went to a place I could order coffee and dry toast. During the time the bread was in the toaster, I went to purchase *The Chronicle.* I sat at a metal table, round, with a smear of coffee.

At the stroke of eight, I went in the elevator to the sixth floor for my paperwork. I then took the elevator to the third floor and sat to wait.

My name was called. I was led to the dressing room where the cubicles have noisy wooden folding doors and lockers with keys that have long plastic tags. I can never make the key work so I place my upper clothing in the locker hoping that and also knowing that no one wants my blouse and bra.

The room with the machine is pink. Bonnie keeps a heating pad, blue background with sunflowers, plugged in. She makes sure that it has warmed the metal plate on which my breast will be placed. The gown I wear is pale blue and ties in front but it must have been designed for a 300-pound woman and so I clutch it closed. Bonnie asks me to remove one arm of the gown and "step up to the plate." The procedure is uncomfortable but my presence is not needed, my body follows directions, and my mind goes elsewhere.

When we are finished with the machine, I sit down on a grey metal chair next to a grey metal table where I have placed my newspaper.

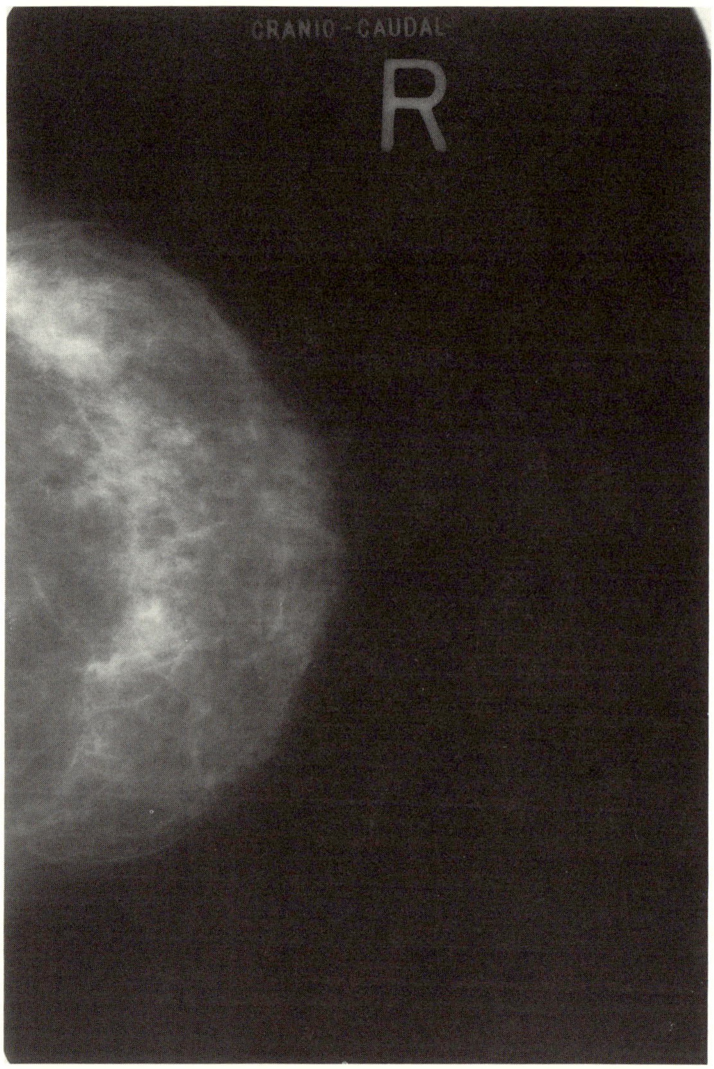

This X-ray will decide my future.

Then begins the wait. What is real, the newspaper? What is being present, looking at the pictures of how to do self-exams on the breast? The truth is my future is on hold. You intellectually realize that this is simply a test that looks at what is already existing but that is not true, not really. You wait for God to decide, for the pictures to be read, for your future to be cast. You read the newspaper and then you don't. It feels cowardly to read and so you sit and wait, and wait and wait.

The door opens and Bonnie walks in, time stops. Then she smiles and says that Dr. Sickles just read the films and everything is fine and I breathe again. There was, you see, that other time. That time the technician came back and said the doctor wanted additional film. Two times this happened. Then she came back again and said that the doctor would like to speak to me. The majority of what he said to me I do not remember. I do remember that he suggested that I go home and have a stiff drink. Two days later a surgeon removed a small malignant tumor and time became a vortex that pulled me into its center. Now, it is seven years later. Bonnie and I walk down the hall, she touches my arm. She understands. I carefully open the unlocked locker, remove the Johnnie, look at my breasts, put on my bra and blouse, and then I walk out the way I have come. I enter the hall with its incredible view of the Golden Gate.

And jump up in the air joyfully and yell "All Right!"

BARBARA WILBUR is a wife, mother, and grandmother. She volunteers full-time, farms, and continues with her love of photography. She is always the student in pursuit of a degree or two and enjoys her "life after cancer."

JOHN M. ROSE

The Mountainside

WE LIVE OUR LIVES on a timeless mountainside with a beautiful, gently sloping valley running down to a cool river. There are many people, a loosely knit community, who live on this mountainside. They live there underneath the azure blue, liquid sky of the bright and beautiful day and beneath the night's indigo sky that floats stars beyond counting. These people weave, throw pots, blow glass, and undertake activities that require the cooperation of many people working together, each offering his or her own particular gifts and talents. Though this population is spread along the gently rolling mountainside, they sing songs to and with one another. One voice picks a harmony to the melody begun by another. They sing sometimes in unison, sometimes in canon. They improvise and then return to familiar strains and improvise again, sharing the joy of hearing their voices spread out and combine in the sweet air.

Also on this mountainside there is a cheap, sleazy, run-down motel. There are definite disadvantages to a traveler checking into the motel rather than camping on the mountainside. Each motel room has something wrong with it. In several rooms the air conditioning doesn't work. In others the television doesn't come on, or it may receive only one or two channels. The television in room 419 gets only the home shopping network. Some rooms haven't seen maid service for months, have no towels, or have dirty towels. As if this weren't bad enough, the man at the office will not let you check into a room as you are. Some rooms allow only an ear to stay in it, and those who get that room must become a huge ear. Other rooms only allow an eye. Thus each room takes only a piece of a person, or,

Opposite:
Wu Wei. *Release of the Crane.* Hanging scroll, ink on silk, 39×74 inches, fifteenth to sixteenth century, Ming Dynasty. Asian Art Museum of San Francisco, The Avery Brundage Collection. Accession No. B71 D1.

if it allows a whole person, they must exist there as a stunted being, never a fully grown adult.

We who travel through life drive up to this valley in our cars, campers, and recreational vehicles and either decide to camp out on the mountainside or check into the motel. Those of us who stay at the motel vary in our degree of awareness of the valley. Some of us become just an eye watching the cartoon channel or an ear at the wall trying to both hear and ignore what our neighbors are doing. Others stand tiny in stature at the window, looking out at the valley and wanting to join those who thrive under the liquid sky. But we are afraid and just look through the window and watch. Those who have taken up their life on the mountainside, on the other hand, sing their songs, especially at night, calling to those of us in the motel to come outside and join them underneath the stars that float in the cool mountain air. To those who can retain an ear with which to hear, the feeling of the song is the same as living outside of the law. They so want to join those who are outside, but they are afraid. Some fear that the stars are too bright, that their tender flesh will be pierced by the starlight. Others are afraid of the supreme vastness of the mountainside, that they will be lost in such enormity. There are yet others who do not even hear the singing at all and are aware of only their motel room. Some valley dwellers come up to the motel and plead in the kindest tone, speaking of how your life can become your own if you simply give up the small security of the motel to live with those who dwell outside.

Others pull up to the motel, find a place in the motel parking lot, and sit in their cars with the engines running, listening to a talkshow on the radio, trying to decide if they will check into the motel or join those who are on the mountainside or in the valley. About those who dwell in the valley, they wonder: Will they accept us? Will they allow us to join and dwell among them? They do not realize that, of course, they will be accepted and taught new ways, and that they too can be part of the vastness of sky, earth, water, mountain, sun, and stars. There is no need to confine themselves to the smallness of the run-down motel rooms nor limit themselves to the diminutive person that these rooms accommodate.

The truth is that our lives beat with two hearts: one with the small heart of the motel room and the other with the immense and vast heart of the mountainside. We can live in either place. It is our degree of awareness, the level of comfort we seek, that makes us decide where to dwell, slipping for moments from one to the other as we grow afraid or tired of the boundary or vastness. Some of us spend our lives skirting the edge between the two, sitting in a lawn chair in front of our motel rooms watching the valley dwellers laugh, dance, and sing. But we can feel either the vastness of our self-boundaries being part of the ecosystem, or the smallness in our bodies, breath, hearts, and minds. Our fear of others who are different from us, our fear of the new and the different, our fear of loss and separation from what we love, or our fear of being tied to what we abhor, are all rooms in that sleazy motel. We have checked into something smaller than we are.

In my vision, I have also learned that death neither stops the beating of these two hearts nor alters the chance of dwelling on the mountain. Time is created by the man at the motel office. When he asks us how long we are going to stay in the motel, we join him in thinking that there are a finite and prescribed number of days we must purchase and spend in his run-down establishment. Outside, however, the days and nights blur together into one wholly present moment. Like a person on an extended vacation, the outside dwellers forget what day it is, even what month it is. Time comes into being which we lodge ourselves in too small a place. It is part of the diminution of our awareness and joins the small stature we must suffer to get into the room. We can forget about time, or harness it, as we change our dwelling place.

Our consciousness is as large or as small as we allow it to be. Death is a boundary that we can choose to dwell within or choose to pass beyond. But with unbounded awareness also comes the fear that we will be lost and not find a place on the mountainside. How ironic—with all the room there is in eternity—that we should fear not having a place of our own when that is all we can ever have. Why should we cling to one moment in time as preferable to any other? Which moment in a life defines that life? Why should death become the moment above all others that defines life? Why should birth? I talked to a man once who lived in the valley. He did not know his birthday, nor did his tribe record the day of his birth. I asked him why he didn't know this day or keep it in his mind. He responded, "Why is that day any more important than any other day of life? It is completely inconsequential." I brought up the subject of birthday presents, and a woman passing by said, "Why should there be a special day for presents? Why any day? Here. Have a necktie."

It is up to us whether our boundaries will be large or small, whether we will include others, nature, or just ourselves, whether we will grimace or sing a song beneath the liquid sky. It is up to us to check into the motel or live with global consciousness as beings of the mountainside.

JOHN M. ROSE is head of the philosophy department at Goucher College, Baltimore.

TONY MITTON

Twelve Gates to the City

[The wall of the city] was of jasper: and the city was pure gold, like unto clear glass. And the foundations of the wall of the city were garnished with all manner of precious stones. The first foundation was jasper; the second, sapphire; the third, a chalcedony; the fourth, an emerald; the fifth, sardonyx; the sixth, sardius; the seventh, chrysolyte; the eighth, beryl; the ninth, a topaz; the tenth, a chrysoprasus; the eleventh, a jacinth; the twelfth, an amethyst. And the twelve gates were twelve pearls; every several gate was of one pearl: and the street of the city was pure gold, as it were transparent glass.[1]

I KNOW OF ONLY ONE CITY WITH TWELVE GATES. It is described by Saint John and by Ezekiel.[2] And, although it grows and changes to reflect the evolving states of humanity, certain features like its gates, remain constant. Both Old and New Testaments say that each of its gates is named for one of the twelve tribes of Israel. It is the City of Man, which shall last while earth and sky endure, for it is founded in the heavens and rooted in nature.

The city's wall is 144 cubits high, and St. John's angel guide emphasized that this is by man's measurement, indicating that this wall represents humanity. The number 144 is the sign for humankind in our souls and personality manifestations. Together we have laid the stones of this wall, building its length and breadth, and for me they represent the transfigured personalities of our lives. They are of jasper, a multi-colored quartz, red, brown, green and yel-

[1] Revelation 21: 18–20.
[2] Ezekiel 48.

low, symbol of beauty and diversity. And, forming the wall, they represent unity.

Ezekiel, writing in the time of the Babylonian captivity, describes a restored home for the twelve tribes. At its center lies an ideal Jerusalem. Beside the city, but not within it, is the temple in a holy area. Ezekiel describes the temple in detail, but gives scant attention to the city which he says is about a mile long and a mile wide. The city of Saint John's vision is greater than Ezekiel's and it has no temple, for the entire city is holy.

I view the New Jerusalem in Saint John's account as mirroring the culmination of humanity's evolving consciousness of God. Moses sees the "I AM" outside himself in the burning bush. Ezekiel places the holy temple beside, and not within the city. Jesus identifies the temple with himself, and tells his disciples, "Who has seen me has seen the Father."[3] And in Saint John's city at the end of time, there is a new heaven and a new earth, and the temple is the human form.

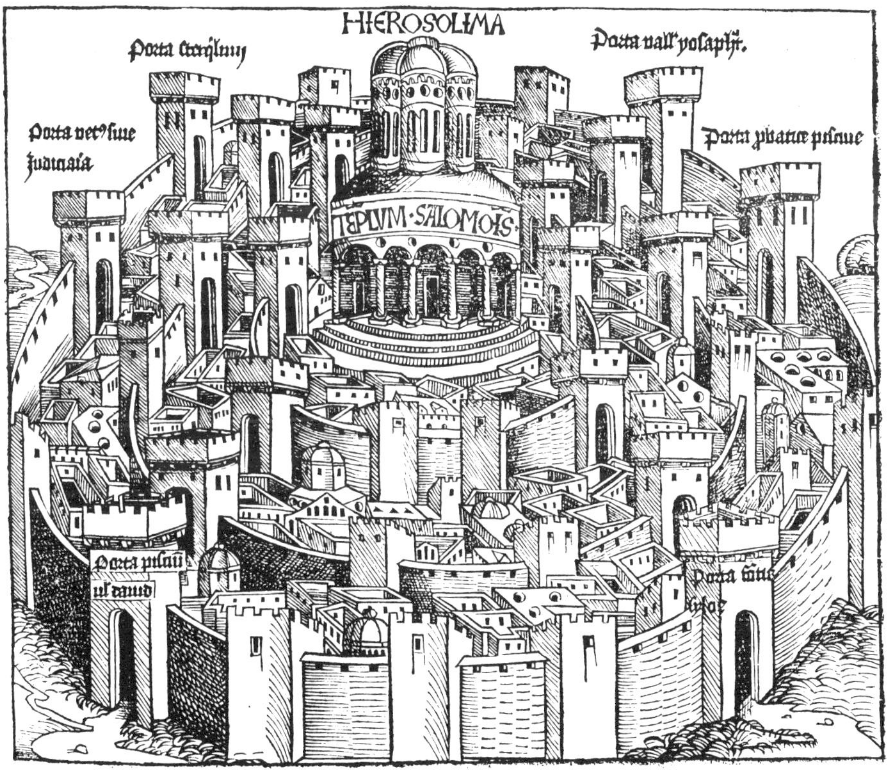

Jerusalem. Medieval woodcut, 1493, *The Nuremberg Chronicle.* New York: The Pierpont Morgan Library, PML 180.

Saint John's city is 12,000 stadia in length, height, and breadth.[4] The number 12 refers to soul configurations, and 1,000 means a vast multitude, indicating that all souls through all time are gathered here. But there is more. The city forms a perfect cube, and it is built

[3] John 14:9.
[4] One stadium is about 607 feet.

of pure gold, "like transparent glass." The cube is the symbol of the material world, and this form, and the spiritual purity and clarity of its construction, carry the meaning that all matter has been spiritualized.

"There are twelve gates, and they shall not be shut at all by day: for there shall be no night there."[5] This text appears to contain at least three separate meanings. First, the city is invulnerable and has no need to close it gates. Second, since day and night are associated with the passage of time, man will have passed out of space/time limits into eternity. Third, since the gates are open, communication and co-creation with other spiritual beings and planes of existence is ongoing. Then, the holy city should not be seen as a place of ultimate rest, but as one where the people co-create with the divine.

Each gate is made of a single pearl. Pearls stand for purity, and singleness for simplicity and in that condition we may pass through them. While still on earth, we may relate to others in touch with the divine, cooperating and co-creating in peace and joy with God; and when all is fulfilled, we shall continue in the city, in love and beauty, wisdom and power, and in the unity of the presence of God. The city is the home of humankind where we may explore the infinite in eternity. Many writers have responded to the Revelation of Saint John, whose vision shows the city in its final state as the New Jerusalem. Emanuel Swedenborg saw the city as a new universal church.[6] All earthly things are representations of a spiritual correspondence. Swedenborg saw this clearly, as did Plato before him.[7] In some sense, earthly cities are imitations, copied well or badly from their correspondence with the ideal spiritual city.

Twelve gates to the city symbolize a comprehensive approach to life and growth. Though order is necessary and theologians have turned to science for help, the scientific method may not be the best tool for examining spiritual and subjective issues. Use of the method means that much data is ignored, and it often leads to conclusions which are at odds with the experience of people seeking to know life's meaning.

There is a complementary approach to thinking which follows a logical path to bring order to ideas, but, like a city with every gate held open, has broader scope. It is the inverse of the usual scientific method, but I believe that for the "soft disciplines," it is superior, providing a set of sign posts for the directions likely to yield productive

---

[5] Revelation 21:25.

[6] Emanuel Swedenborg. *The Heavenly City: A Spiritual Guidebook.* Translated by Lee Woofenden. West Chester, Pennsylvania: Swedenborg Foundation, 1993.

[7] Cyriel Odhner Sigstedt. *The Swedenborg Epic.* New York: Bookman Associates, 1952. p. 178; New York: AMS Press, Inc., 1971.

research.[8] Whereas objective science builds its hypotheses on controlled, measurable, and replicable studies and tends to dismiss other evidence as anecdotal, the alternative method accepts as does an open door all evidence: including myth and art, religion and archaeology, physics and psychology, and so forth. Any evidence is acceptable until it is shown to be false. An advantage of the holistic method is that it gives weight to a volume of evidence, even if laboratory controls are lacking. The criterion is convergence with core data, though possible contamination by outside influences must always be investigated. Thus, much anecdotal evidence can be considered, and so can personal experience, though here we must be particularly aware of distortions produced by our own psyche. The nature of the holistic method, however, is to check all such observations against each other, as well as against all other evidence. While bias is probably unavoidable, it is likely to be identifiable and even capable of correction.[9] This central core of data is formed organically, arising from the nature of the evidence itself, and not by external design.

We may call it the holistic method representing the different gates of learning. It uses a macroscope and synthesizes, whereas objective science uses a microscope and analyzes. The method has a natural tendency to resolve differences, even controversies, for it reaches out to related core data to find common ground. This method incorporates evidence ranging from the ancient east to Rudolf Steiner's contemporary spiritual science. These form part of its core of information, along with the data of medical science. This extra-disciplinary evidence suggests that the human being is actually a composite of bodies operating on different planes of existence.

Comparing Ezekiel's vision with Saint John's, we can see that though the city changes and grows through time, it is always perfect. This is illustrated by a movie I once saw, taken of Picasso while he was drawing. The design on the canvas was "in place" from the very first line. His process of creation added meaning as he worked, but the form behind the hand was always there. He probably had a mental image of the essential elements before he ever set chalk to canvas. Art is a spiritual process, and I take this to be an example of how we

8 A soft discipline is an academic term, often used pejoratively, to distinguish sciences where exact measurements are difficult or impossible from those where the laboratory setting is the norm, e.g., psychology is "soft" and chemistry is "hard."

9 The holistic method does not subscribe to the law of parsimony. In this method, a hypothesis will appear more valid than others through the clustering effect of the data itself. In this, it is superior to parsimony which has never been more than a methodological convenience, and has been abused to justify the dismissal of valid data because it did not fit an accepted paradigm. The holistic method is information hungry, both for depth and diversity. The more that is stored in the brain using it, the more likely that it can be used productively. It is above all a tool to deduce basic principles and thus suggest the lines along which further research should proceed. The next step might be to formalize the range of information necessary to make up the method's information core. Of course, such a step would never be complete but always capable of expansion.

co-create with God through time, and how the work is always perfect in eternity.

In studies of religion, spirituality, and mysticism, the holistic method is unsurpassed, for it does not question assumptions, but tests them against each other, as well as against data from other fields of study. By validating participants' experiences from within, it allows the student to approach the inwardness of an issue.[10] The holistic method may help us towards a better understanding of the concepts of freedom and responsibility, which at the intellectual level appear to be in opposition. At that level, the idea that what we must do is what we most want to do, may seem like an imposition. Yet, if we meditate on the idea, it may become actual experience, since energy follows thought. Then our whole perspective may change, for we have approached the frontiers of the spirit and what seemed like an imposition is experienced as joy.

Consider a holistic method to approach the twelve-gated city. The core evidence indicates that there is a beneficent Creator who is both transcendent and immanent in all things, and that there is an evolving consciousness in man. For man, the guiding rule is the same as for the Spirit, *freedom with responsibility.* Man is now returning to the unity of the spirit with his creator. In his return, the key role is played by the Christ, a concept present in all religions. Other core evidence suggests that there are many planes of being besides the physical, that thought is the creative force of the universe, and that there is a universal principle of correspondence, as above, so below. All things are interconnected, and man is the microcosm of the macrocosm. Let us see what evidence resonates with this core.

In sacred texts, the reference to numbers is never casual. There are twelve gates, and the completed city of Saint John is 12,000 stadia long, broad and high. There were twelve tribes of Israel and twelve apostles. There were twelve labors of Hercules and in the heavens stand the twelve signs of the zodiac, which astrologers from ancient time have claimed to have vast influence on man: ruling the nature of civilizations over long epochs, as well as influencing individual soul configurations and personality attributes.

There is a view which sees human life as woven into the different zodiacal experiences in a complex variety of ways.[11] Each life pre-

[10] "Understanding the inwardness" was a favorite phrase of the late Lord Boyle, former Vice-Chancellor of Leeds University and arguably one of the best minds in British Cabinets in this century.

[11] Guenther Wachsmuth. *Cosmic Aspects of Birth and Death.* Ghent, New York: Golden Stone Press, 1988; Paul Platt. *The Qualities of Time.* Vols. 1-5. Ghent, New York: Golden Stone Press, 1986–1992; Robert Powell. *Hermetic Astrology.* Vol. 1, *Astrology and Reincarnation,* 1987, and Vol. 2, *Astrological Biography,* 1989. Kinsau, Germany: Hermetik.

sents its own challenges and leads on to the next. In this view, the occurrence of the number twelve in any significant context would suggest some relationship to the evolution of Man on Earth.[12]

Cities have gates, and gates have two aspects. They invite the traveler to enter, but they also make the city vulnerable, and so must oppose the ill-intentioned. One gate remains out of those built in ancient time, when men still sought to copy spiritual correspondence. This is the Ishtar Gate of Babylon, and it may be seen in Germany at the Pergamon Museum in Berlin. Six times the height of a tall man, set with glazed tiles of brilliant blue, awe-inspiring and overwhelming, it offers both an invitation and a warning. This gate is not only a defense against armies, it is a portal of spiritual initiation, and on its threshold stands a guardian.

The traveler does not approach the gate casually. The avenue through which he walks is lined on either side with tall statues, of lions and of a dragon-like creature which resembles a griffin. On the universal plane, the opposition of lion and griffin reflects the basic dualism of human nature. The interaction, friction if you will, between soul and personality is the means by which we learn and progress towards the unity of the spirit. "DK," source of the Alice Bailey books, has said that the motto of humanity is harmony through conflict.[13]

If it were not a traffic impediment, I sense that the avenue of statues would have been built as a rising stair, with a step between each pair. It would mirror the necessary raising of consciousness preparatory to crossing the threshold. For me, that has been achieved by all the minor initiations, insights, and experiences, like windows opening on the soul, which I have accumulated through life. There have been confrontations with both lions and griffins, as when science tempted my reason, asserting that its progress would explain all things; and reason responded that life seemed a universal principle. Where life was, there was evolution too. Other openings have led me toward the gate. I realize that no action undertaken out of fear of consequences has any moral value; I hear the answer in my mind, "All is of Me," when questioning a certain spiritual discipline; and I learn how this is so, recognizing in the *Course in Miracles* that my function is to forgive, so that by the grace of God, sins are not and mistakes never were.[14]

---

[12] The sequence of the twelve Buddhas is significant to human evolution, because the Buddhas are entrusted with making the spiritual breakthroughs from a human direction. Guatama achieved compassion, and Maitreya will achieve love, in grateful, loving response to the Deed of Christ.

[13] Alice A. Bailey. *A Treatise on the Seven Rays.* New York: Lucis Publishing Co., 1962.

[14] *A Course in Miracles.* 3 vols. Tiburon, California: Foundation for Inner Peace, 1975.

As I stand before the Ishtar Gate, I realize that this is a personal journey. Advanced on either side, the flanking towers rise up to dwarf me, huge, glowing with color, dominating in their strength. This is the gateway of my soul. I sense that I am but a step or two from the threshold. The Guardian who awaits me may be my greatest fear. But if I understand that the children of God need fear nothing, then the Guardian becomes my friend.

Above my head rises the archway of the Gate. The physical configuration of the arch is such that it raises the personal aura of the individual who passes through. Thus emperors raised arches to celebrate their triumphs—Titus, Constantine, Napoleon. But such archways pass from empty space to empty space. The arch at the Ishtar Gate is more than this. It serves as the guardian of the city, to impress the city's purpose and nature on all who come there. Just so, the Gate of the New Jerusalem will impregnate with its holiness the traveller who acknowledges the angel on its threshold. For citizens of the true city are people in touch with the divine.

TONY MITTON received a master's degree in economics at Cambridge University, England. His background is diverse including public service on the Birmingham City Council and five years at the Findhorn Foundation in Scotland. He has lived in many parts of the world and speaks four languages. Currently he is a planner for a state agency in Florida. Tony says his spiritual orientation is eclectic and pragmatic.

PART II

You Need a Walking Stick

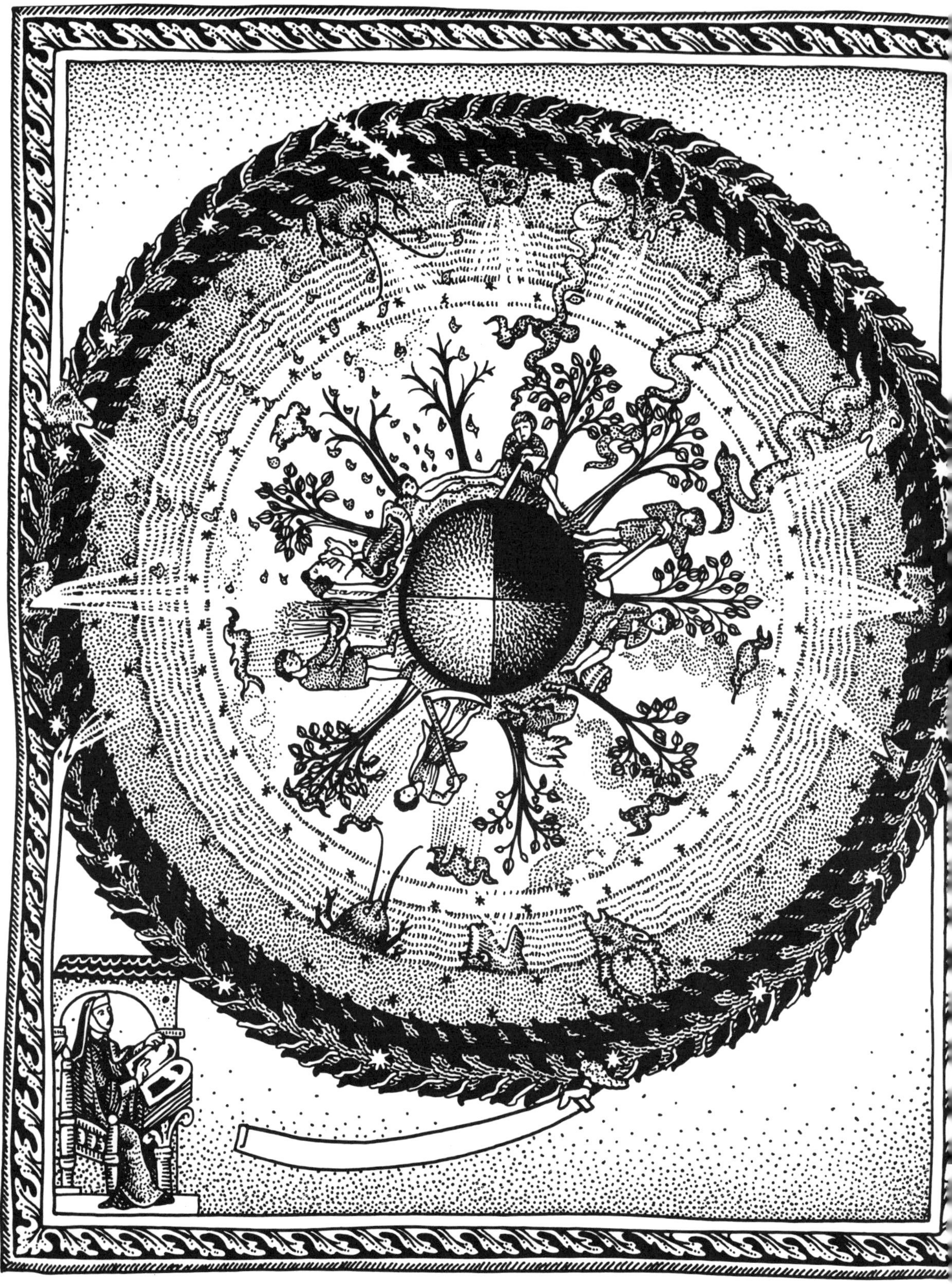

MARY KAY MCKEON KLEIN

Hildegard of Bingen

It happened that in the eleven-hundred and forty-first year of the Incarnation of the Son of God, Jesus Christ, when I was forty-two years and seven months old, Heaven was opened and a fiery light of exceeding brilliance came and permeated my whole brain, and inflamed my whole heart and my whole breast, not like a burning but like a warming flame, as the sun warms anything its rays touch. . . . I had sensed in myself wonderfully the power and mystery of secret and admirable visions from my childhood—that is, from the age of five—up to that time, as I do now . . . the visions I saw I did not perceive in dreams, or sleep, or delirium, or by the eyes of the body, or by the ears of the outer self, or in hidden places; but I received them while awake and seeing with a pure mind and the eyes and ears of the inner self, in open places, as God willed it.

—HILDEGARD OF BINGEN[1]

Opposite: *On the Articulation of the Body [Cultivating the Cosmic Tree]* from Hildegard's fourth vision in *Hildegard of Bingen's Book of Divine Works.* The illustration was originally drawn by a contemporary of Hildegard. This rendition is by Angela Werneke, published in *Hildegard of Bingen's Book of Divine Works,* edited by Matthew Fox. Santa Fe: Bear & Co., 1987.

HILDEGARD OF BINGEN, twelfth-century mystic, found her gate to the heavenly city by accepting visionary gifts received from God and using those gifts to lead, inspire, and teach her contemporaries as well as readers in succeeding centuries. Her recognition that she was nothing and God was all, and her at times painful search to hear what was being asked of her, resulted in an extraordinarily effective and productive life.

Born near the Rhine in the year 1098, Hildegard was the tenth child of Hildebert, a German knight, and Mechthilde. Her family was

[1] Columba Hart and Jane Bishop. English translation. *Hildegard of Bingen: Scivias.* New York: Paulist Press, 1990.

wealthy, and she was considered to be of noble birth. At the age of eight, she was sent to live at Disibodenburg under the tutelage of Jutta von Sponheim, the daughter of a count. Jutta was a holy anchoress who instructed Hildegard in prayer and religious life. It is not known whether her parents were aware at that time of her visionary gifts. She lived a quiet life, praying, working, and being faithful to her call. Hildegard joined the Benedictine group in 1113, when there was already a community at Disibodenborg. After Jutta's death in 1136, Hildegard was chosen to become abbess.

In her forty-second year, after experiencing the opening of heaven and its warming flame of life, Hildegard resisted the call to write and had fallen ill until, with the help of a monk, Volmar, who transcribed her visions, she wrote *Scivias,* which literally translated means *Know the Ways.* According to scholars Columba Hart and Jane Bishop, in this work, Hildegard describes and comments on her visions, which deal with the theological issues of creation, redemption, and sanctification.[2] Later she wrote *Liber Vitae Meritorum* (1158–1163), a work on ethics, and *De Operatione Dei (On the Divine Works,* 1163–1173), which reflect her mature vision of God and creation. In 1158, she suffered a prolonged illness, and then began preaching, which was most unusual for a woman in her time.

Her outer life was at times marked with disharmony. After she became head abbess of the convent in Disibodenburg, she decided that the group was too large for its small quarters. Hildegard and her sisters' departure for Rupertsberg in 1151 caused much controversy. The monks did not want to see her leave because of her reputation and because the dowries of the sisters would go with her. Later Hildegard founded a second convent at Eibingen, across the Rhine from Bingen.

Developing proficiency in many areas, Hildegard was a gifted composer of the music that her sisters chanted in liturgical services. She was also a poet and healer, as well as a scientist. Her preaching emphasized the corruption of the Church.

Hildegard differs from other women mystics; her writing is not "intensely devotional, erotic, and ecstatic" but is focused on "the cosmic dimension, the struggle between good and evil, an absorption with the great work of redemption and the role of human beings. . . . She does not present herself as a role model or lay down a path of mystical union for others to follow. Hildegard is, rather, a mouthpiece, a 'small trumpet', 'a feather on the breath of God', whose task is to teach and correct her fellow men and women and to glorify the Creator."[3]

---

[2] Ibid., pp. 22–23.

[3] Fiona Bowie and Oliver Davies, eds. *Hildegard of Bingen: Mystical Writings.* Translated by Robert Carver. New York: Crossroad Publishing Co., 1995. p. 21.

I became interested in Hildegard as I researched important figures in the history of Western spirituality for a course I was planning to teach at the Swedenborg School of Religion. I have had an interest in Swedenborgian theology and spirituality for many years, and was looking for similarities and differences between Emanuel Swedenborg's work and that of other Western mystics. I had first encountered Hildegard as a result of reading Matthew Fox's work on creation spirituality. I found myself identifying with some of her struggles about accepting her call, and with the joys and sorrows of her work as abbess.

What is important to me as a twentieth-century woman is the model of faithfulness to her call, as well as her understanding of the heavenly city, and her gate into it. Understanding one's call and responding to it can be extremely difficult at times, and Hildegard experienced both the difficulties and blessings of this process.

Three themes in Hildegard's work are particularly important to me: her cosmological awareness, through which the light of God shines in all that is in this world; her sense of the reality of good and evil; and her acceptance of her prophetic call, which enabled her to see clearly what needed to be done and to accept the sometimes harsh criticism that came her way.

Cosmological Awareness

Having been raised in an urban area in a society that has often seen the natural world as an object to be conquered rather than part of an ecosystem in which we all participate, I have been a long time coming to an awareness of the presence of God in all of the natural world. Reading Hildegard has helped me with the growth of this awareness: she has a "special intimacy with the natural world," and was "not attracted to the divine in its pure transcendence as many mystics are."[4] This point is well illustrated in Hildegard's letter to Bishop Eberhard II of Bamburg; the letter speaks to the unity of creation in God's spirit in which "no creature, whether visible or invisible, lacks a spiritual life."[5]

Many of Hildegard's prayers reflect on the beauty of the cosmos and God's presence in it, as in the following example cited by Uhlein.

> Without the WORD of God
> no creature has being

[4] Gabriele Uhlein. *Meditations with Hildegard of Bingen.* Preface by Matthew Fox. Foreword by Thomas Berry. Santa Fe: Bear & Co., 1983. p. 13.

[5] Matthew Fox, ed. *Hildegard of Bingen's Book of Divine Works, with Letters and Songs.* Santa Fe: Bear & Co., 1987. p. 281.

God's WORD is in all creation,
visible and invisible

The WORD
is living,
being,
spirit,
all verdant greening,
all creativity.

All creation
is awakened,
called,
by the resounding melody,
God's invocation of the WORD.[6]

Themes from the Gospel of John—such as the nature of creation, God's love for humanity, and "the light that shines in the darkness"—were very important to Hildegard, as can be seen in this prayer. Matthew Fox speculates that life in the lush Rhine valley may have contributed to her view of greening power as the power of life, the power of God.[7]

Cosmological themes are central to many of Hildegard's most famous visions. Advocates of creation spirituality, who affirm the goodness of God, God's loving presence in creation, and the unity of science, religion, and art, find Hildegard a mystic who inspires and informs their insights. Matthew Fox, a leading proponent of creation spirituality, often cites Hildegard as a precursor of the creation spirituality movement. In Vision Three of the first part of *Scivias,* for example, Hildegard sees the firmament in the shape of an egg. The image exhibits wholeness and interconnectedness, the potential of new creation, new life. As Fox comments, it shows the universe as "living, breathing, growing, surprising, renewing, loving, embracing, creating."[8] In the later *Book of Divine Works,* Hildegard adopts the more common view of the time that the universe is a sphere, but the same feelings remain in her vision.[9] In the Fourth Vision in *Divine Works,* "On the Articulation of the Body," she saw God's presence in the cosmic wheel of the elements and seasons. Humans cultivate the earth and nurture its productiveness in a universe in which God's presence radiates.[10]

---

[6] Uhlein, *Meditations.* p. 49.

[7] Matthew Fox, ed. *The Illuminations of Hildegard of Bingen.* Santa Fe: Bear & Co., 1985. pp. 30–33.

[8] Ibid., p. 36.

[9] Fox, *Book of Divine Works. p.* 35.

[10] Ibid., pp. 80–148; Fox, *Illuminations.* pp. 46–49.

Preparation for Christ, from the seventh vision in *Hildegard of Bingen's Book of Divine Works.* The illustration was originally drawn by a contemporary of Hildegard. This rendition is by Angela Werneke, published in *Hildegard of Bingen's Book of Divine Works,* edited by Matthew Fox. Santa Fe: Bear & Co., 1987.

Hildegard expressed cosmological awareness in letters as well as in meditations on her visions. She wrote the following to Bertha, a German noblewoman who married the Emperor of Byzantium, and became Queen of Greece and Empress of Byzantium.

> God's spirit breathes and speaks: in wintertime, God takes care for the branch that is love. In summer God causes the same branch to be green and to sprout with blossoms. God removes diseased outgrowths that could do harm to the branch.
>
> It is through the little brook springing from stones in the east that other bubbling waters are washed clean, for it flows more swiftly. . . .
>
> These lessons also apply to every human being to whom God grants one day of the happiness and glowing sunrise of glory. Such a person will not be oppressed by the strong north wind with its hateful foes of discord.[11]

[11] Fox, *Book of Divine Works.* p. 292.

Reality of Evil

Hildegard's awareness of life, creativity, and the greening power of God is tempered by her awareness of the reality of evil. This, too, has been important to me; even though the cosmos is full of the presence of God, we do not live in a purely good world. In my view, any vision which does not take into account the reality of evil cannot adequately describe our universe and our lives. Some of her most moving passages involve the description of Lucifer's fall from good:

> The numberless cluster of sparks clinging to the first lost angel was reflected in the splendor of his total beauty in such a way as to fill the world with light. But that angel, who should have felt an obligation to serve with his great beauty, the Deity, turned away from God's love and toward the darkness as he rose up and said to himself: "How splendid would it be if I could act according to my own will and accomplish the works I see only God accomplishing." . . . And at once that angel fell, together with his followers, down into the place of darkness described above. Like a lump of lead he fell. Yet he still thought he could fight against God, whose works he could not behold shining in the darkness.[12]

The contrasts between the light of God and the darkness, service to God and the will to act on one's own, appear throughout Hildegard's work.

Hildegard's images of greenness and moisture also relate to the contrast between good and evil. In the Seventh Vision of the Third Part of *Scivias*, for example, Hildegard contrasts moisture with the drying up attributable to sin.[13] Hildegard's vision in her forty-second year also shows the light/darkness imagery. When she responded to the light and to the call to service, her illness was healed. The images of light and moisture are always associated with the vitality and love of God, whereas darkness and dryness signify the absence of that life.[14] Dryness and evil are real; we are in need of redemption and of opening to the love of God that fills us with life and moisture.

> Now in the people
> that were meant to green,
> there is no more life of any kind.
> There is only shrivelled barrenness.
>
> The winds are burdened
> by the utterly awful stink of evil,
> selfish goings-on.

---

[12] Fox, *Book of Divine Works.* p. 88.
[13] Fox, *Illuminations.* pp. 63–65.
[14] Fox, *Book of Divine Works.* p. 38.

Thunderstorms menace.
The air belches out
the filthy uncleanliness of the peoples.

There pours forth an unnatural,
a loathsome darkness,
that withers the green,
and wizens the fruit
that was to serve as food for the people.

Sometimes this layer of air
is full,
full of a fog that is the source
of many destructive and barren creatures,
that destroy and damage the earth,
rendering it incapable
of sustaining humanity.[15]

Prophetic Sense

Hildegard had a strong prophetic sense; even though the stands she took were unpopular and unacceptable to some, she responded from her deep commitment to what she believed to be right. In the introduction to *Scivias*, Hart and Bishop made the following comment on her prophetic role:

> Although the abbess could inspire deep loyalty and devotion in her friends . . . . her sheer force of will, combined with a dazzling array of spiritual and intellectual gifts, a courage hardened by decades of struggle, and a prophetic persona, which she displayed in season and out, made her a formidable opponent.[16]

Having been through some painful moments in my own life when I felt compelled to take a strong stand and suffer the consequences, I admire her strength and commitment.

Hildegard preached on the corruption of the church and wrote to popes and other prominent figures to express her views.[17] She founded religious communities, sometimes with much opposition, and began a "political–mystical movement" in the Rhineland that led Matthew Fox to call her the "grandmother of the Rhineland mystic movement." This movement included Francis of Assisi, Mechtild of Magdeburg, Meister Eckhart, and Nicolas of Cusa "all of whom brought the powers of mysticism to bear not on supporting the sta-

[15] Uhlein, *Meditations.* p. 77.
[16] Hart and Bishop, *Scivias.* p. 15.
[17] Fox, *Book of Divine Works.* pp. 269–362.

tus quo but on energizing the prophetic in society and church. For Hildegard, justice plays a dominant role in her cosmos, her psychology, her theology of work and morality."[18] Though not a feminist in the contemporary sense, she supported women in their struggles for respect and justice.

Hildegard's letters, in much the same vein as the vision quoted from *Scivias,* show her to be a person who tried to be open to God's word and to respond to the prophetic call. In several of her letters, she shares some marvelous imagery on this point. In a letter to Wibert of Gembloux, she writes:

> God works where God wills, for the honor of the divine name and not for the honor of earth-bound mortals. But I am continuously filled with fear and trembling. For I do not recognize in myself security through any kind of personal ability. And yet I raise my hands aloft to God, that I might be held by God, just like a feather which has no weight from its own strength and lets itself be carried by the wind.[19]

Hildegard was very strong in her support of Elisabeth of Schöngau, a visionary who was concerned and upset about people's response to her visions. Born in 1135, Elisabeth was a Benedictine nun who wrote several visionary works. Two letters from Hildegard to Elisabeth are extant. Hildegard writes to encourage her:

> I am but a poor creature and fragile vessel; yet what I speak to you comes not from me but from the clear light. Human beings are vessels God has made and filled with the Spirit so that the divine work might come to perfection in them. For God does not do things the way we humans do. It was through the divine Word of command alone that everything came into existence perfect....
>
> Those who long to bring God's words to completion must always remember that, because they are human, they are vessels of clay and so should continually focus on what they are and what they will be. They should leave heavenly things to the One who is heavenly, for they are themselves exiles who do not recognize what is heavenly. They only announce the mysteries like a trumpet which indeed allows the sound but is not itself the source that produces the note. For someone else is blowing into the trumpet and causing the note to be produced.[20]

Hildegard supports and consoles Elisabeth and encourages her to see her gifts as a means of service, as Hildegard herself did.

Hildegard had a long and successful career as abbess and founded another community at Eibingen in 1165. She had preached and

[18] Fox, *Illuminations.* p. 17.
[19] Fox, *Book of Divine Works.* p. 348.
[20] Fox, *Illuminations.* pp. 338–340.

written on many topics. But at the end of her life, Hildegard was involved in a painful incident. In her last year she had to take a stand for justice that cost her personal peace and silenced the music of her convent. A young man, described as a revolutionary, had been buried on the convent grounds. He had been excommunicated by the archbishop, but Hildegard insisted that he "had confessed, been anointed, and communicated before dying."[21] She refused to throw his body out of the cemetery. Her convent at Rupertsberg was placed under interdict, and the sisters were not allowed to receive communion or to sing. The interdict was lifted shortly before her death in 1179. It was typical of Hildegard to stand by what she felt was right and absorb the consequences of her actions. Hildegard writes movingly in the *Divine Works* about the satisfaction one may feel with old age:

> And just as the greening power and the flowering as well as the ripening of all fruits come to an end in winter, we also fade away at death along with all our good and evil works. Those of us, however, who have performed good works in our childhood, maturity, and old age will mount up with our soul to God, radiant in our good deeds and as if adorned with jewels. And the body by which the soul has done all these things will scarcely be able to wait until both body and soul are together again in the abode of joy.[22]

Faithful to her vocation, Hildegard was anticipating entrance into the fullness of the holy city to which she had been led through her special gifts, and which she had sought in all the years of her earthly existence.

[21] Ibid., p. 8.
[22] Fox, *Book of Divine Works*. p. 113.

MARY KAY MCKEON KLEIN is president of the Swedenborg School of Religion and has had a long-term interest in the writings of women mystics. She received a doctorate in philosophy from Boston University and has taught philosophy, interdisciplinary studies, women's studies, and spirituality, in addition to performing her administrative work at the seminary.

ANNE MARIE MACARI

Julian of Norwich

. . . but all will be well, and all will be well, and every kind of thing will be well.

SHE'S SEALED INSIDE THE WALLS OF THE CHURCH. Through the stone's squint she hears the world whispering.

Who watches her? Who kneads her bread and brings her water now that she has disappeared under His cloak? Who picks the pocked fruit by her doorway, or brings her honey and tiny nuts, forever patient in their shells?

She watches rotting pods fall from the wet trees. Childlike questions keep coming, multitudinous, out of their sulphury eggs. Visions embed where her lips have pressed them.

If only we could see what she sees. Even the worst of it. Woody thorns, copious blood. Her sight fixed on the cold walls, her body stiff and aging before us in the quivering light, the tight room crowded with outstretched intermediaries.

Now all she has prayed for presses her unmoving to the bed.

Isn't this more than she ever wanted? This stilled life, these visitors, their blue breath dancing from their open mouths.

ANNE MARIE MACARI has been published in *Field* magazine. She is at work on a novel about the Middle Ages and lives with her three sons in Mt. Kisco, New York.

JENNIFER LEONARD

Magic Encounter

I WAS TEN YEARS OLD, I couldn't read, and going to school was a cruel ordeal. I could recognize certain words, I could write them by copying them, but the secret of reading was unrevealed. This came about because I first attended a progressive school in New York City, a place where the children were free to encounter learning when they were prepared and some inner prompting led them to sit down and be taught in little groups of two or three. I detested the school, its dingy rooms with windows looking toward brick facades with their own dark windows. I longed for the light and liveliness I'd been born to in India. I was an American child whose scientist father was doing research on tropical diseases, whose mother relished the fading days of the raj, and I had played happily with the servants' children and lived secure in the ever-present protection of my doting ayah. This life ended abruptly with the outbreak of World War II and, paradoxically, by coming to the United States I became a refuge.

My alienation from New York, from the noise and the climate, from the children in the school, seemed a physical barrier that wrapped around my small but entire self. I retreated into silence and what was probably despair. My withdrawal was interpreted as slow development, and I was left alone.

The next year found us living in Delaware and I entered second grade. No progressive school this, students read from first grade on; I pretended to read and for the next three years I was the worst student in my class and a complete failure in the eyes of my parents and myself. Each day of school was agony, each weekend a state of fast-fading grace, each summer a short lifetime of reprieve. There were manifestations of my despair and humiliation: I rarely went to sleep before midnight and I suffered from desperate shyness. But this is not a recitation of my psychological state. It's the story of a consummate and compassionate teacher, Miss Susan Blauvelt, a wise woman.

Hudson River Landscape. Artist unknown. Oil on canvas, 25¾×19¾ inches, ca. 1840. Providence: Musem of Art, Rhode Island School of Design. Gift of Mrs. Murray S. Danforth.

Miss Blauvelt was eighty. She had been a schoolteacher from the time she left her training, sixty years before, which is not to say she was still teaching, but she was still a teacher. The first day she opened her door to me there were seventy years and my illiteracy between us. She was a little bird of a woman with a sweet voice that was nearly a chirp as she asked me in. Her hair was in a schoolmarm's bun, her face was deeply creased, her clothes were a long skirt and a shawl with trailing fringes. I stood before her speechless, looking at her honest eyes, seeing in their light an acceptance and an open understanding. Little did I know it then, but when she closed the door behind me I had stepped into a new world, the empire of the written word.

At the time Miss Blauvelt and I met, I was in fifth grade, living in Nyack, New York, a little town then, on the western palisades of the Hudson River. The palisade is comparatively gentle in Nyack, but even at that the houses seemingly leaned toward the great Zee at this point in the river. It had been my fifth grade teacher who had discovered that I couldn't actually read; it was she who informed my shocked parents and arranged for my tutoring with Miss Blauvelt. Each afternoon after school I walked to her little house, which was on a street that ended with a seawall beyond which stretched the wide river. I came to relish my walks to her home, as they always included this lovely view of the river, a kaleidoscopic world of color and illusion, a ceaseless modality; and then abruptly I would be in her old-fashioned living room where another magic reigned.

After our cups of tea we would sit at her carved desk, side by side, turning the pages of a very old reading book. My mind would become completely still as my concentration deepened. I would gaze and gaze into the book, into the words, into the letters as Miss Blauvelt spoke softly, pointing here and there, turning a page, working the slow alchemy of her teaching into my mind. In the ebbing light of those fall afternoons she transformed my fear and doubt and despair into a glimmer of understanding, then growing comprehension and then bumpy ability; and then suddenly, in one instant, the transformation occurred, I could read, I knew it, not the sounding it out, not the hesitancy and uncertainty, but the full realization of reading. We laughed.

There is a mystery in this moment in learning when the subject is transformed from a set of tools, clumsy and awkward to wield, into fullblown comprehension in which the tools are abandoned because the grace of the matter is revealed completely. Miss Blauvelt understood this mystery. She probably could not predict its moment of arrival but she knew it hovered just beyond the boundary of perception and she knew she could bring about that encounter between the student and enlightenment. Her teaching was an act of skill and patience, gentleness and faith as she shepherded my incomprehension to the point where it would encounter this mysterious revelation, where the dross of a halting mind was consecrated by knowledge.

The leap from the illiterate to the comprehending is almost unfathomable, or was to me, who experienced it so much later than my peers. My world regained the sun; books that were once impenetrable blocks of words became panoramas; reading was my Cinderella's slipper.

Many years later, when I became a teacher of literature, I taught to bring my students to that revelation that comes by true reading, when one can see beyond the two-dimensional print and into the heart of the words, into the images of wonder as they have been designed by our creative masters. There is more to reading than scanning a page for casual or uninvolved comprehension; there is a transformational process of dynamically engaging one's mind with an author's. Miss Blauvelt taught me this, she taught me to be courted by words, to have a love affair in the dimension of the angelic intelligences. She brought me to light and life as surely as my parents gave me a body to contain my soul. As Archimedes said, "Give me a place to stand and I will move the world." Miss Blauvelt, in her small living room, at her little desk, gave me a place to stand, a place where I would be courted by Dante, Virgil, Shakespeare, Homer, Milton, the poets and prophets of generations; and I took possession of their ideas, those vibrantly colored living ideas that enliven life and support the soul's invincible surmise.

JENNIFER LEONARD is a writer, teacher, and reviewer for the Chrysalis Reader, for which she researches facets of its themes as they touch the heart and the literature of the Western tradition. This story was published in the Summer 1986 issue of *Chrysalis: Journal of the Swedenborg Foundation*, under the title "Where Another Magic Reigned."

ROBERT FLAHERTY

Dreamgates

While we sleep we are not concerned with bending the outside world to our purposes. We are helpless, and sleep, therefore, has rightly been called the "brother of death." But we are also free, freer than when awake. We are free from the burden of work, from the task of attack or defense, from watching and mastering reality. We need not look at the outside world; we look at our inner world, are concerned exclusively with ourselves.

—ERICH FROMM, *THE FORGOTTEN LANGUAGE*

WHILE I WAS PASTOR of a rural church, I once drove four teenagers in my car to a youth retreat. At first the kids talked nonstop, shifting quickly from one topic to the next—kids at school, teachers, couples. And of course, they talked and giggled and sang traveling songs.

When the conversation died down and a more reflective atmosphere settled in, I suggested that each of us share a recent dream. In turn we all did. We laughed because much of the imagery tickled us. And we talked—some about our laughter, some about the more weighty issues of our lives. I never expected teenagers to share in the depth they did, especially not with an adult. Their dreams gave them a springboard into some significant issues.

One girl recalled a recurring dream.

> I am at a beach playing in the sand. I dig a hole with my little play shovel and put the sand into my bucket. Then I fall in the hole. Only the top of my head is above the level of the ground. I reach up to pull myself out, but instead I pull in handfuls of sand and dig myself deeper into the hole. It scares me. I can't get out.

The girl was one of my congregants. I knew her family and her living situation. Although she feigned not to understand the dream, it shouted to me because it represented her situation so perfectly. She lived with her maternal grandparents, who eventually adopted her.

Earlier her father had abandoned her and her mother was unable to care for her. The grandparents provided for her needs and cared deeply for her. Still they had a hard time realizing that their granddaughter was a maturing young woman. They kept a tight reign on her. She felt smothered. Sometimes, like a window into the soul, a dream lets you clearly see a person's life, including your own. In this article, I have used dreams, my own and others', to show how dreams offer insight, which in turn offers a person new ways of understanding life, and sets one free to live differently.

My own dreams have been as revealing to me as the young woman's above. I shared the following dream in a workshop:

> I was at a meeting where I met an attractive teenage oriental girl. She took a liking to me at her mother's prompting. I hugged this girl, wishing I were her age and could make a meaningful connection with her, but I knew I couldn't. "I'm 35, married and have four children," I said. [At the time I was not 35 and I did not have four children.]

Before the session, I had worked on the dream. As an experiment in dream interpretation I treated the dream as an allegory and translated the symbols into an interpretive narrative. The recast dream sounds like this:

> I'm at a discovery point in my life. Oriental religions and philosophy attract me. Eastern history and tradition especially allure me. I want to embrace their truth, but I realize it is so different from where I am that the power of my own past frustrates my desire. "I'm steeped in my own tradition and it has borne its fruit."

One woman who knew me, hearing the dream shout its message just as I had heard the teenage girl's dream, interrupted my talking by saying out loud, "That's Robert!" My dream clearly pictured what was going on inside of me. I first shared this dream in a workshop over ten years ago.

A SERIES OF THREE DREAMS, occurring over several months, brought to light the shadowy "male" assertive side of myself.

1. I am coming out of a conference talking with a tall black man in a shabby dark blue overcoat. Someone else joins us and I introduce this man as a friend of my daughter. I know I am lying. (The dark shadowy male side of myself is my friend, but I am not willing to publicly own him.)

2. I am down in the dark cellar of my home looking for something. Suddenly I am aware that there is a man near me. I am terrified and I wake myself up, literally shaking. I decide I need to go back down into my unconscious and find out who he is. But I will not go without something to protect myself. I decide to take a croquet mallet.

(I do not get back into the dream. This shadow figure, unknown and unseen is very frightening. Still, as a weapon, I choose something that could also be used for play.)

3. In the third dream, I am waking up very early in the morning. It is spring, I climb a hill to where I am having a house built for myself. As I get there, I realize there is someone upstairs in the unfinished house. I yell at him to come down out of there. As I stand outside, frightened, a male friend in back of me laughs. A ruddy young man comes out the door—he is the carpenter.

(As I work with the dream, the young man—my male shadow self—coming out into the morning sunlight is like Mercury or Hermes. He is a trickster god who guides the traveler between heaven and hell. Mercury is also an alchemical element used to change dross metal into gold. A year later I recognize the carpenter as the divine within me: Christ building my house as I slept.)

—PERRY MARTIN

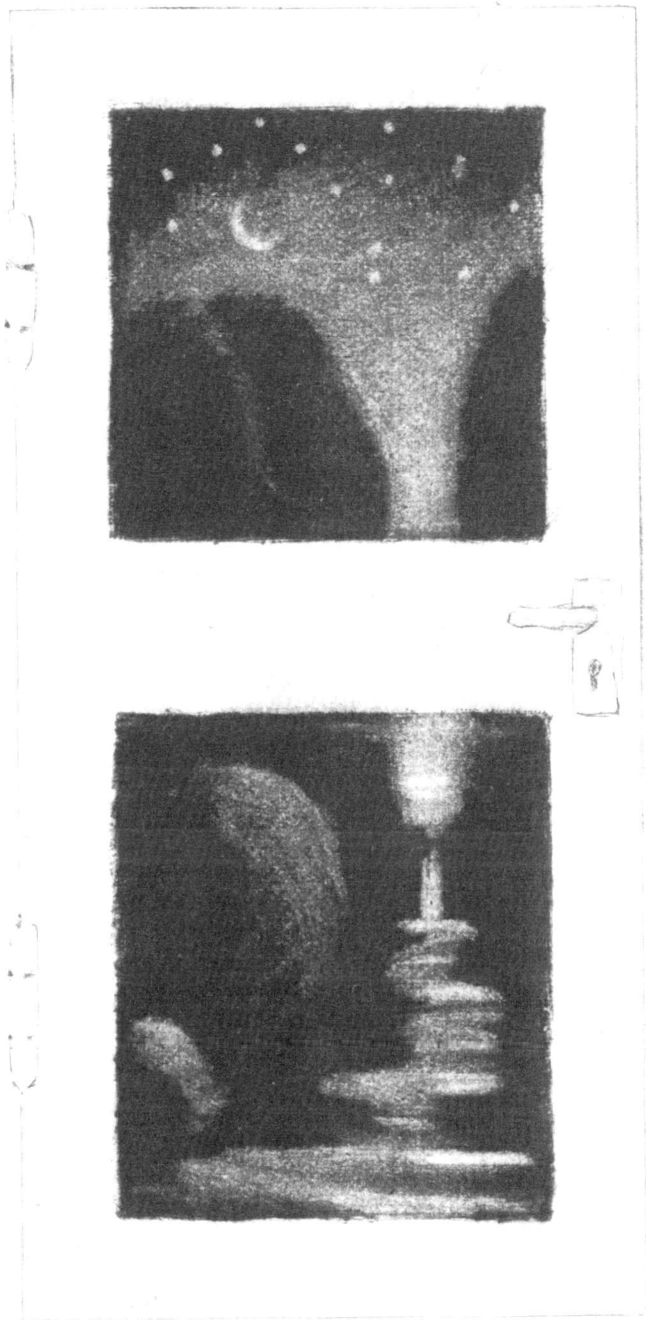

Sven Widén, *Night's Door.* Mezzotint and dry point (black-and-white), 4×8 inches, 1988.

During the intervening years, my attraction to Eastern thought has grown, and I have found significant ways to make the connection.

Indeed, dreams are windows through which we see ourselves. Even though sometimes the view is clear, we may need time to accept what we see. For instance, I worked for two years with a woman who initially complained of depression that she rightly attributed to an unhappy marriage. During our time together she learned to accept the reality of her married life and discovered in which direction she might move to improve that relationship.

In order to use your dreams, you must ask questions of them and of yourself. I gave her a copy of Ann Faraday's book, *The Dream Game.* Between sessions, she read the whole book. From then on she recorded her dreams with more confidence. Since we had a shared vocabulary to talk about dreams, such talk became a significant part of our sessions together.

The following is the first of two cycles from her dream journal. The first cycle brings her problem to the fore. And the second shows her resolution.

> January 12—The dream: I was in the washroom in the basement, looking at all the dirty clothes I had to wash, hanging up on the clothes line. I noticed my daughter's jumper. I thought, I have a lot of ironing to do!

Her comments about the meaning: I have a lot of ironing out of my problems to do. I also have a lot of washing (problems) to work on.

> February 24—The dream: I've got a baby girl in my arms. She has soiled her diaper and I want to bathe her. I draw the water and try to put her in, but she cries. It's too hot. So I keep running cold water until the bath is cool enough.

Her comments about the meaning: I am in "hot water" about my marriage. It is very messy.

> March 10—The dream: My husband's niece died. I was waiting for the girl's mother and father to visit us. I had picked up the boots and shoes in the hall and swept the dirt. Then I realized they wouldn't come, because particularly the father was too upset to visit.

Her comments about the meaning: I feel dead inside. Have "tidied up" some dirt. Maybe I need to have some fun. My niece, the little girl, represents fun. It is gone, dead.

> April 7—The dream: My husband had given away or sold my Ford Fiesta. I was furious.

The dreamer's comments about the meaning: No more fiestas (parties). Do I feel sold out? My husband doesn't want me to move or grow.

THESE DREAMS USE PICTORIAL LANGUAGE, weaving several motifs together into one message. Laundry is one of those motifs. The dreamer recognized it as a pun in her interpretation: I have a lot of washing (problems) to work on. Dysfunctional families often have a rule that their members will not "air their dirty laundry in public."

This short dream made the same statement twice. The dreamer interpreted ironing to mean she had to iron out her problems. In other dreams variations of the motif come up. The dreamer needs to wash a dirty diaper in hot water. She needs to tidy up her house for the sake of visiting relatives—her husband's relatives at that. These dreams led to conversation that led to acknowledgment that her marriage was dysfunctional. Although she knew this at some level, not to talk about it made the dysfunction a secret, something hidden from plain view. Keeping the dysfunction a secret gave the dysfunctions power to bind the woman. But when the dream brought the dysfunction into view, it lost its power. The dreamer was on her way to freedom.

Equally vivid and repeated in this woman's dreams is her lack of joy. The image of her niece reminded her of her inner child and that it was dead. And her dream punned with her about having fun. Her husband, the destroyer of her fun, took away her fiesta.

Her dreams clearly gave a repeated message, the troubled marriage robbed her of fun. What is so significant about that? The dream does not provide the answer. But now the dreamer had a way to talk about the mess of her marriage and her lack of joy. That is a significant gain.

Before her dreamwork, when she talked about her marriage, she said she had no feelings other than guilt. She blamed herself for the trouble in her marriage. One dream gave her a clear picture of where the trouble lay:

> I AM SOMEPLACE IN THE ORIENT. There is a large orange sun and a Japanese gate, closed. I'm sitting on the ground waiting.
>
> The emotional coloring of the dream is patient anticipation and a lack of anxiety.
>
> Shortly after having this dream, I saw an opportunity to go to a gestalt therapy and Zen meditation workshop in Japan. The workshop was reasonable, but getting there was extremely difficult. I thought about it and thought about it and continued to have the dream. Finally, despite my fear of airplane travel, I went. It was in Japan that I was introduced to Zen practice. Prior to this my spirituality was dormant. I am a Franciscan, Anglican. I now call myself a "Zen" Christian. I had this repeated dream until I went to Japan, then the dream stopped. The gate to my spirituality opened.
>
> —ELLA MARIA MORA

> May 13—My sister-in law was playing a piece of music at the piano for her husband, my brother-in-law, who was listening.

She interpreted the dream as a picture of herself and her husband. Then in her journal she asked the rhetorical question: Do I feel my husband would change if he'd listen to me?

The second cycle of dreams illustrates that the dreams not only helped the dreamer to define her problem, but also helped her to reframe the situation.

> June 24—The dream: I was standing on a quay watching a battleship sail away, behind it a landing ship. Someone was standing with me—maybe my daughter.

The dreamer's comments about the meaning: The battleship represents my husband, the landing boat, my son, and the quay, the key to my problems! Putting it all together she writes: I feel the key to our problem is that both my husband and son move out and I can take care of my daughter. A sudden change of interpretation, without warning follows: Maybe I'm the battleship!

Other dreams of this period repeated the message. This retelling of the story made it possible for the dreamer to integrate the story into her life and to act on it. On July 25, she moved out. Still the dreams continued to show the dreamer her life.

> 19 December—I moved into an apartment with my daughter. Another woman was sharing it with me.

> 31 December—The dream: I had composed a new melody with my own hands. Someone told me I was doing well as I played it on the piano.

Her comments on the meaning: I can see that I am reshaping my life and that is good for me.

As in the first cycle, so in the second: repeated images came together, especially music, song, composition. Hope, joy, and creativity came back into the dreamer's life. Dreams had certainly opened a window into her life. And so she wrote:

> Dreams have helped me to get close to myself—to see my worst and my best sides. They have helped me to see what was going on in my heart, and guided me in my decisions. They have shown me how much pain I've been feeling, my anger, my hopes and fears, and helped me to see my need for fun.

Still, the meaning of a dream is not always so obvious or the dreamer misses a deeper meaning at first. For that reason, coming back to a dream, taking a fresh look at it brings new insight. The ambiguity of pictorial language allows many interpretations. Pictures stimulate other images that in turn stimulate still others. And with each image we make associations. This chain of pictures and associations leads us to interpretation.

Thomas Moore, in *Care of the Soul,* tells how he encouraged a woman to take a second look at her dream. She related a dream "in

I SEE A LARGE OAK TREE in the center of a large field covered in snow. There is a broken fence. I climb over and walk toward the tree. When I get to the tree, I see it is full of snowy owls. I reach up and they walk up and down my arms. I feel very excited, curious, not afraid, they look deeply into my eyes. The largest one walks up my arm. He feels very heavy. He looks at me and then says he has a gift for me. He places two tiny baby owls in my hands and tells me I must nurture them until they are grown and hide them and keep them safe until they are grown. I agree and as I walk away with them, the one in my right hand turns into a serpent and bites me until the blood runs down my arm. The pain is excruciating. I hold on and take them home. The owl on the left bites me also. At home I build a place for them. Many people, including men like FBI agents, come trying to find them but I avoid them and then I wake up. I feel powerful.

Message—I can survive anything and feel powerful about myself.

I had just returned to college at the time of the dream seventeen years ago, and I was apprehensive of what might be ahead. The dream gave me courage and peace of mind.

In the American Indian culture, Snake people are very powerful because they have survived the bite of the serpent. Owls are transitional, messengers of change. Owls can be interpreted as death.

What I was aware of was that changing myself is not as difficult as learning to use the knowledge I already have in a wise way. The owl represents to me the changing of the self. The snake the need to learn wisdom.

—CONNIE LUNDGREN

which she has absentmindedly left her front door open, allowing a man to sneak into her house."

"It was a nightmare," she says. "I think the dream is telling me that I'm not careful enough about keeping myself protected. I'm too open."

Accepting an interpretation too soon or making it too final closes the door to other possibilities, to other ways of seeing. Moore continues: "You see, I'm given a dream and an interpretation. . . . It's so reasonable. Of course, she is too vulnerable and is threatened by an intruder."

Then Moore looks at the image from another angle. What else does it suggest? He asks the dreamer to reconsider the opening in the door. "Maybe it's not so bad," he tells her, "that your usual thought about closing doors failed in this case. Maybe it allowed an entry that would prove to be beneficial. At least we can keep an open mind."

Moore concludes: "Speaking for other figures in the dream, sometimes against the bias of the dreamer, can open up a perspective on the dream that is extraordinarily revealing. . . . Other characters may need acceptance and understanding." *

Since picture language invites us to look again, to ask what else can I see, I wondered what would happen if I returned to a dream a couple of times. So I tried. Here is the dream:

> A little girl was lost. I had the feeling she had drowned. The last time I saw her, she was wearing a blue plastic jacket that looked much like a life jacket with ripples running up and down.
>
> I was standing next to a police car parked by the water's edge. Police radios were blaring and people were moving about chaotically. The police found a piece of blue plastic. They thought it was a clue to finding the girl. Since I had an interest in her recovery, they showed me the piece and questioned me. I tossed the piece on the seat of the patrol car and told the captain in charge of the investigation that what he had handed me was not part of the girl's jacket. It was a piece of a swim fin.
>
> The captain was angry with me and treated me as a "hostile witness." I wondered how I could turn his opinion around.

A month after the dream, I worked on it. Immediately I linked the little girl with little Red Riding Hood, who suggested innocence, trustfulness, and unwariness, especially in the face of danger. Naively I have entered situations in which I am surprised that people have hidden—even vicious or malicious—agendas. Am I failing to acknowledge such a situation now?

Another image, the little girl's drowning, brought back a memory from my childhood. While at a church camp, I was swimming

*Thomas Moore. *Care of the Soul.* New York: HarperCollins, 1992. pp. 293–294.

with my cousins. From the high dive, I could see my cousin (wearing a blue bathing suit) underwater near the edge of the beach. I knew something was wrong. I screamed for help, dove into the water, and swam as quickly as I could to the shallow water calling for help all the way. By the time I got there a lifeguard was pulling my cousin out of the water. She never recovered. The people around her brushed me aside. This association caused me to ask, what part of me is trying to assert itself or gain attention?

A third image, the police, represented an authority outside myself, who pointed the way, but who picked up on the wrong clues. This action reminded me of an incident that occurred only a few days earlier when I tried to share with a fellow chaplain the dynamics of the way I process events in my life. In certain situations a strong need to excel, to be perfect, will drive me to replay events obsessively, trying to make them right. Although I want to, I cannot stop myself.

When my colleague asked about the beginnings of this behavior, I rehearsed a litany of experiences. After a short conversation, in the standard jargon of a counselor, she suggested I had not "worked through it." I resented her lack of appreciation. Like the police officer, she picked up on the wrong clue.

Finally, the anger with the police captain put me in another bind. In the dream itself, I wondered how I could make the captain like me and include me in the investigation. While working on the dream, I wondered who owns this investigation. Of course, in the dream the police did, but I wasn't happy with the direction of the investigation. I wanted to be in charge. The desire to gain the captain's approval and the desire to be in charge plunged me into internal conflict. What would it cost me?

SEPTEMBER 28, 1994

I am on the edge of the business district in the northern part of town, of either my current city or that of my childhood. I am in the middle of the road. There is a church over on the right and a school bus in the parking lot with yellow warning lights flashing—why? It's not waiting for passengers. It's just holding a space for someone? A group of people on the other side of the street—on the corner—are having a religious debate.

I hear organ music. Is it coming from the church to my right? Someone may be practicing. It sounds like the Wagner wedding march. It becomes louder and I see as it passes us from behind that it's being played by a black man in an open convertible. He's holding the steering wheel with his left hand and playing (one finger) a keyboard on the dashboard. It must be a synthesizer of some sort to sound *so much* like a full pipe organ. I expect to see a bridal party following him, but the group that follows him is something else. It's a parade of children, walking in the street, but not marching in a rigid way.

I hear the words and I realize that it's *not* the wedding march but a Christmas carol, "O Come, All Ye Faithful." The children are mostly pre-teens and *not* any really young children. I see (or am told) that one of the girls is crying. I think it's because of the beauty of the song.

—MILDRED LAAKKO

So these were my musings on the dream at my first look. I laid the dream aside for another month, and then picked it up once again for another look. What did I see that second time?

First, the searching struck me as important work. Although I knew what I was looking for, I could not describe it accurately enough for someone else to find it for me. When the captain showed me what the police found, he expected I would claim it was what I looked for, but I did not. Once again I felt myself in a bind. I wanted the captain to like me, but I could not concede my search. Next I asked myself, who is the little girl? The child in me; my feminine side, my anima; something precious that needs protecting; a lost or drowning part of me.

Identifying with the little girl led me to ask, where am I in the dream? I am an observer who wants to find the little girl. I am also a reporter—the police captain called me a witness. I am also a judge or critic, evaluating the investigation and the way the police are carrying it out.

Finally, I turned my attention to the police captain. Who is he? An outside authority, my superego, my parent. As soon as I thought of the captain as my parent, I knew I was using transactional analysis jargon. The girl represented a child. In my search for the child I was the nurturing, caring parent. And the captain was a domineering parent. Differing aspects of myself were fighting with each other. Both wanted to achieve good ends, but fought about what the ends were and how to achieve them.

Taking a second look, in fact, brought new insight. Dreams speak their message in pictures. As you look at the pictures, they may immediately shout their message or they may more subtly reveal their meaning later.

ROBERT FLAHERTY is an ordained United Methodist minister serving as an army chaplain. He has conducted dream workshops for personal growth and often uses dream work in counseling. PERRY MARTIN, PH.D., is a psychotherapist in West Chester, Pennsylvania. She does dream therapy as a part of her mind/body integrative practice. ELLA MARIA MORA, M.A., a certified specialist in mental health, has taught in several colleges and universities, and has led workshops in personal growth for twenty-five years. As a lay Franciscan, she offers spiritual guidance, and is in private practice in Seattle. CONNIE LUNDGREN is a certified marriage and family therapist. She specializes in and advocates therapeutic work with young children. This work has taken her to Lithuania for the past three summers, leading training on child advocacy, adoption, child abuse, and prevention. MILDRED LAAKKO is pursuing a degree in occupational therapy.

MILES ROBINSON

Thoughts While Shaving

Who is this
disguised
with ever deepening
wrinkles? Every year the cartilage
softens a bit more, the once
delicate nose becoming
a beak, the man of flesh
yielding to the man
of bone. Gentle
cheekbones protrude, whites
of eyes deepen
to old ivory.

Beneath, self-awareness
grows, sensitivity now
unmasked, secrets
uncovered one by one.
The sower of seed still
answers the calling,
but beyond the mirror
lies the far field.

MILES ROBINSON is a retired electronics engineer and attends the University of Maine, Augusta, where he studies art and English.

NEIL S. STEFFEY

Tsunami

(for Amy)

There is a chair that is
a window and a
soul that is a
beach to place your
naked feet against.

Redwoods gaze
against the bay, a
stubborn pocket of green,
a valley you visit
beside the sweeping waters. . . .

I am eighteen forever
again and smell
again the secrets
in a storm, touch
the long gray sky
in swallows,

the earth you straddle,
the pillowed chair
you're floating in
just now,
beside the window,
soaking elsewhere

in the wet struggle
of constant weathers,
in love again
and moist
with it.

NEIL S. STEFFEY is an adjunct instructor of English at Butler University and the University of Indianapolis, and the Poetry Fellow at Butler University's Writers' Studio. He has been published in *Sycamore Review* and *Painted Bride Quarterly*. *Tsunami* is a Japanese term for tidal wave.

LORETTA JURAS

The Guide Who Listened

In the history of everyone in whom the artist-within has survived conditioning, schooling, training, there are persons, influences that have kept him alive, awake, who have encouraged him without even trying—just by being. They have been one's real teachers.

—FREDERICK FRANK

PEACE DID NOT COME TO ME UNTIL I WAS SIXTY-FIVE and a newly discovered antidepressant from India came on the United States market. Resolving my biological imbalances enabled me to open myself to a state of mind where I could begin to process a lifetime of disappointments. At that very time, I was fortunate to find a Franciscan priest guide. He had a quick intellect and listened fast. Instinctively I knew there would be no need to interpret for him the world of emotional turmoil: transference, suppression versus repression, clinical depression, and so forth. All I had to do was reveal myself to him. Father would understand and guide me.

My first appointment was on a beautiful sunny day in mid-December. Father greeted me with a big smile and a warm hug. It was easy sharing despite my rush to show him, in a composite way, what my life had been. I had become quite adept at reviewing and summing up my life's experience.

For more than forty years, I had searched every avenue for help: religion, psychotherapy with four different psychiatrists, analysis with a psychoanalyst, spiritual guides, medicine, philosophy, literature, poetry, the Psalms, travel, support groups, various occupations, studies in abnormal psychology and sociology, and even spending three years in a convent.

What's it like to be depressed? If you have ever had the experience of being *lost* when you were very small, recall the fear of feeling utterly alone and abandoned. That will give you an inkling of what depression is. You watch life going on in people all around you; but you are not part of that life. You are, as it were, *disconnected.* Real things are all around, but nothing has meaning for you. That's the impenetrable wall that surrounds you. You simply *hang on* to that little bit of you that's still there, and wait till the worst part of fear subsides. Then you might be able to come out of the nightmare by focusing on the beauty of the sky, the singing of the birds, or the flowering trees.

My guide was a good, understanding listener. He never interrupted. In a little over an hour, I had shown him much of my background right up to the present. Since I would only be seeing him monthly, I began sharing through writing. The more I wrote, the

Opposite:
Giorgio de Chirico,
The Seer. Oil on canvas,
27½×35½ inches, 1915.
New York: The Museum
of Modern Art. James
Thrall Soby Bequest.
(Photograph ©1995
New York: The Museum
of Modern Art.)

more I remembered traumatic childhood events. During most of my life, I had been too depressed to allow myself to remember these suppressed or buried events. I had all I could do to focus on the problems of the day. Now, I could "unload" by sharing with my guide events of years back. I think one has to look back before moving ahead. In the past, my help had been analytical. With Father, I could describe my emotional life and then put my life together, synthesizing it. It was so easy to reveal these things to Father. He was the only one I ever told about not bothering my parents for twelve dollars for a graduation ring; that I didn't love my father; that he was unable to "be there" for me; that I couldn't believe in God, but I was trying. There would be other secrets in the months to come; how upsetting for instance, it had been when I left the convent.

Father reawakened in me my love for books and the ability to find help through reading. I would share my discoveries with him. When I discovered the poetry of Emily Dickinson, I found tremendous comfort in it. I gave Father a volume of her poems. He was delighted with it, and wondered why he had not read from her before. She, too, had difficulties with traditional faith. Her writings reflected her extremes of utter disbelief.

Her mystical poems inspired me to express myself in poetry. The following poem tries to capture one of my lowest moments.

Depression

Loneliness is a hunger;
A gnawing, burning cry.
It destroys from within;
No food can satisfy.

It rages like a fire—
A fear that will not end.
Body and soul are consumed—
For the want of a friend.

A spiritual guide can help one find her place in the universe; can help her reach for God. Spiritual direction has been compared with towing a boat on a straight course versus rowing round and round in a circle. I told Father how I always begged God to take away my terrible scared feelings and loneliness. Father told me the story of the little child who was afraid of the dark. His father called to him not to be afraid because God was always with him and would protect him. The child replied, "Can you send me somebody with skin?" I became aware that I was very angry about a God who had not heard the pleading of a girl no more than ten or eleven. If God existed, all powerful, why had he looked the other way and allowed me crushing disappointments and dashed hopes again and again?

What kind of god was that! I complained to him: "Here I was, less than twelve years old, frightened and clasping a small crucifix, begging God to take this thing (depression) away from me. I had no other place to turn. Why didn't God help me?"

Father said quietly, "I only know that God is always with you and that He loves you." I thought of a poem by Emily Dickinson:

> I never saw a moor,
> I never saw the sea;
> Yet know I how the heather looks,
> And what a wave must be.
>
> I never spoke with God,
> Nor visited in heaven;
> Yet certain am I of the spot
> As if the chart were given.

Intellectually, I can understand my problem. As I told Father, the only medicine I could tolerate didn't come on the market until 1993. It supplied the chemical my brain lacked—much as a prosthesis makes it possible for one to walk without legs. However, emotionally, the scars are still there. No wonder faith and love were sadly lacking except for the rare heights when I was experiencing the beauty of nature and the arts. His kind acceptance of me was of tremendous importance; his presence provided spiritual solace. The more I shared with Father, the more I was able to share.

On a better day I told Father I sometimes think of God as magic. I can't see God, but there are times when I can *feel* the Presence of God; the *ultimate* feeling. I just know it has to be God. There's no way to explain this magical, all-absorbing experience. I think of God as being the magic you find in a child's eyes or in a beautiful rainbow. That *magic* just happens. You cannot cause it to happen. It comes when it will. Rejoice in that moment and recall it afterwards. Father liked my analogy and encouraged me to pursue this kind of thinking. This living in the present moment may be what Lao-Tse meant when he wrote:

> As rivers have their source in some far-off fountain, so the human spirit has its source. To find this fountain of spirit is to learn the secret of heaven and earth.

A FEW DAYS LATER, while I was doing some journaling for myself, I realized what it was about Father that made him so special, so helpful. He was genuine! He wasn't just doing a job. He was real, like a friend who is there for you when you need him. It's easy to share things and not feel degraded in the process. Father really listened. Once, he started to speak but stopped immediately because I went right on talking.

Looking back, it seems to me that Father may have never known how much his saying nothing, nothing at all, was just the right thing. His attentive listening helped me more than anything he could have said. It was not Father's nature to sit back and listen. He was known for his ability to speak well, to think on his feet, and was an active, in-charge type. Months later he would confess: "They tell you to say nothing when you don't know what to say." Shortly after this, Father was called to another parish. I never had another conference with Father. But I will be forever thankful that I was blessed to have a spiritual guide who listened when I was coming out of the depths of despair. Father was my "somebody with skin."

TODAY, I CHOOSE TO FOCUS ON THE INFINITE, the eternal. I choose to spend time with God, with thoughts of God, and his goodness, and loving care for me. I'm growing . . . thank God. For a change, I'm beginning to see Godlike qualities in myself, instead of worshipping the Godlike qualities in others. As I grow to accepting and loving myself, I'll find out more about God and will be able to love more.

Now I am able to enjoy life. At last I'm free to read whatever and whenever I wish. My condo is bright, sunny, and cheerful. There are plants and flowers in abundance. Classical music plays in the background. I experiment with cooking and have occasional dinner guests. I'm learning to play bridge. It's easy to relax, and I even take an occasional nap.

Tuesday is my volunteer day, and I love what I do. As a Eucharistic minister, I'm privileged to take the Eucharist to medical and surgical patients at the hospital where I worked for so many years. In the afternoon, I spend an hour or more with a group of fifteen to twenty nursing-home patients. I give them all the same loving attention that I gave to my mother in her last years. We converse, sing, and pray. The final twenty minutes is reserved for a particularly uplifting reading or video.

Wednesday mornings I sing with the Blue Rocks, a chorus of forty women. We rehearse for concerts eight months of the year. Twice a year we give nine concerts in nursing homes, churches, and retirement homes. Music has strange powers. Music goes beyond words and calms the soul. It heals and gives new life to the depressed.

The weeks fly by and the dark cloud of depression no longer hangs over me. I am grateful for my health, my life, and my friends. I experience exhilarating moments when I watch a spectacular sunset or listen to the song of the birds. I am resolved to make each day count as I drink in the early violets, the morning glories still wet with dew, and all the beautiful forms of creation. When September comes, I shall once more register for interesting courses given at the nearby Academy of Life-Long Learning.

LORETTA JURAS, a retired health care worker from Wilmington, Delaware, graduated from the University of Delaware and continues to take courses and volunteer as a Eucharistic minister. She is currently writing a book about her life-long experience with clinical depression.

CORRINE DE WINTER

Twins

In the womb you were
like Narcissus by the lake
absorbed in fascination.
Three minutes separated you at birth.
Mama brought you into the light
where she made mental notes
(one had a birthmark
the shape of Tennessee)
and often sang sweet tales of wonder.
The first thing you remember
is her voice close to your faces
whispering: My son, why are you so
beautiful? You could not ask
which one did she mean
but even before
you could play with your twin brother
you knew you had
fallen in love with each other.
Your tender faces
tiny pale lakes
yearning to reflect.

CORRINE DE WINTER has lived in Massachusetts all of her life. Her poetry has been published in *Common Journeys* and *Ellipsis*. Corrine enjoys nature and photography.

PART III

On the Path

BARBARA CASEY

A Frog on the Threshold

WITHOUT ANY ADVANCE WARNING that there was a problem, my husband one day suddenly began experiencing delusions and hallucinations. Over the next few days he heard voices where there were none to hear. He saw people and things when there was no one or nothing there. His confusion was constant.

The doctor diagnosed his condition as a stroke or another disorder, something that could be determined only after extensive medical tests. Whatever the outcome, there was little hope for recovery. The doctor's words were devastating and heartbreaking. And not only was my husband's life shattered, but the life we had shared was broken with it.

When we returned home that day from the doctor's office, I found a frog, sitting on the windowsill in my bedroom. It was one of those whitish-looking ones with a big lean body and bulging black eyes. Not wishing to share my home with it, the only other choice I had was to capture the thing and release it as quickly as possible outside. Armed with a much-too-small towel, I chased the frog off the sill, around the dresser, across the floor, and up the wall while my husband watched with a child-like curiosity. I finally managed to confine it within the folds of the towel.

"Run, open the front door, darling, will you please?" I asked my husband, hoping that he would understand the urgency of the situation and do as I asked. Mercifully, he did. I rushed outside and immediately threw the towel into the nearest flower bed. In a few moments, the frog disengaged itself from the towel, and somewhat nonplussed, hopped toward the shade of the nearest ixora bush.

Later that night I awoke to find that my husband was not in bed. Frightened that he might have wandered away from home, I snatched up my robe and slippers and ran outside. There in the moonlight I saw my husband standing in the flower bed where I had released the frog earlier.

"What are you doing?" I asked.

"I don't know who that guy was," he answered, "but seeing how you treated him this afternoon, I didn't want to take any chances."

The next day my husband was scheduled for an MRI (magnetic resonance imaging), the first of many tests he was to go through during the next two weeks. There was no mention of the frog incident, but he could no longer bear to have me out of his sight. It was as though fear of losing me had moved into that part of his mind where our shared reality had once lived. He followed me from room to room in our home as I got ready to take him to his appointment at the Regional Medical Center. During the thirty-minute drive, he continuously reached out to touch me—my hand, my dress, my face, my hair—as though to reassure himself that I was really there.

Once we arrived and the preparations for the MRI were started, he became alarmed that I might not be in the room with him during the actual procedure. The possibility of my not staying with him during the forty-five-minute test was not even an option for him. When the nurse suggested I might be more comfortable in the next room, my husband became so agitated she didn't mention it again. Instead she brought me a chair to sit in and a hospital bed sheet as a cover to keep from getting chilled in the cold room.

During the test I sat at my husband's side, talking nonstop so he would know I was there and not move. I talked about how we met, how wonderful his influence had been on my two daughters and how well they were doing in their chosen careers. I talked about all the trips we had made and were planning to make. And I talked about our love for each other. I did not talk about the frog.

We somehow made it through the test, but that night another problem developed. My husband had been troubled with chronic swollen prostate for some time, but it suddenly became enlarged to the point where he could not urinate. At two o'clock in the morning I drove him to the emergency room where he was catheterized. Surgery was scheduled for later that day. We returned home only long enough to pack a few of his toiletries before returning to the hospital. I stayed with him in the receiving room where patients are prepared for surgery. I walked alongside the orderlies as they rolled him into surgery. When I started to leave he became so upset he tried to climb off the gurney and come after me. So I waited with him in surgery until the anesthesia took effect.

Once my husband was in recovery, the doctor came to get me so I would be there when he became conscious. I stayed with him, sitting on a wobbly metal stool, until he could be moved into a room. By now it had been over twenty-four hours since I had slept. In the early evening my husband was resting comfortably. A nurse brought up a dinner tray for me from the hospital cafeteria so I could eat with him. When at last he drifted off to sleep, I drove home, only taking time for a hot shower before falling into bed.

The phone startled me awake at 1:35 AM. It was the night duty nurse, and she couldn't control my husband. He was yelling and trying to get out of bed so he could find me. I quickly dressed and drove back to the hospital where I spent the next two days and nights, sometimes sleeping on the floor next to my husband's bed, or in a chair pulled up close enough so he could touch me. After the second night, a catheter had to be used again, and finally we returned home.

I helped my husband into bed and, totally exhausted, I lay down beside him, pressing my body next to his, my arm draped over him so he would know I was there. At 3:30 in the morning he said my name. He told me to watch for the frog. And he told me he loved me. Then he died.

Later the medical examiner explained that he had died of a heart attack. I was overwhelmed by the shock and suddenness of it all. But now, with the passage of time, I am working through my grief. And whenever I see a frog in my garden, I smile.

BARBARA CASEY is the author of two novels for children, and her poetry and stories for adults have appeared nationally in magazines and newspapers. Barbara is the Florida Regional Advisor for the Society of Children's Book Writers and Illustrators. DIAN MCCARTHY is a Maryland artist.

PATRICK KANOUSE

Gone to Oregon

To the memory of Walter Jameson (1913–1995)
and Glenn Kanouse (1913–1995)

Waking, my eyes, and in the night
My soul, seek you. Overcome
By my body, in my lonely bed,
I see you beside me, lying,
In the lying visions of sleep.
You would conquer sleep
If you really came to me.

—PETRONIUS

1994

Congealing heat, in pools across the road's
Horizon, marks my last destination—
The rhythm of each piston and yellow
Hyphen blazes my trail westward, where land's
Horizon ends and sea's begins, across
The continent's broken anatomy:
Its veins, spine, and callouses. Oregon,
Whose green cliffs lick the sea, to you I go
In search of the end search, of breast and shroud.

One one thousand, two one thousand, three one . . .

1931

Coal-grime gathers above Peoria,
Slowly sinking, yellow-pitting grey walls,
Cursing the lungs. Two hundred prayers all for
One job; four hundred hands searching pockets
For stray hopes: Who is the blessed one? Off
The coast of Gaul, Caligula struck his
Sword against the sea and wiped Neptune's brine
Back, claiming godhead.
                                        In the silence of
Grime and factory's pulsing grinds, rumors
Spread, thesis becomes law—A job! a job.
Hitchhiking to Indianapolis
The next day, I gamble; hundreds pray for
One job; no stray coins—I'm the lucky one.

. . . thousand, four one thousand, breathe, one one thou . . .

1994

The stars tenaciously puncture the night's
Catacombs, whose rhythmic breathing unfolds
The limitless to the drowsy eyelids.
God breathed soul into the earth, Icarus
Succumbed to ecstasy, and the rondure
Of the city's midnight light witnessed the fall—
I feel the sky's grain and grind and pulse; its
Subtleties lost among chasms of star
And star, star and earth.
                                        Vulcanized rubber
Scars the pavement, the city's glow subsides
To memory and enjoins my voyage
West, where the moon echoes on the ocean.

. . . sand, two one thousand, three one thousand, four...

1920

Four feet above the Illinois River
There was freedom:
                                Raw hands unclasp the rope.
For a moment, I'm outside gravity's
Noose, where ersatz wind and sounds of somewhere
Peoria clutch my hair, I found flight—

Later, among alluvial rocks, I
Found an arrowhead dulled by steel bullets
More accurate—its eroded delta
A symbol unknown to me, its plight

A surety.
Three inches from the shore
Of the river, freedom joined water's tomb.

. . . one thousand, breathe, one one thousand, two one . . .

1994

Strange patterns emerge from the inconstant
Onslaught of billboards, stuttering dos and
Fees—other patterns, a conglomerate
Of headlights, trees, and distant homes (mute with
But bracketed silhouettes)
—And the stars

Pass obscurely—
And patterns collide, my
Voyage mocked, my search justified—stars pass
Another city's glow withers to thought.
Patterns rescind the epic.
I'm alone.

Moon-studded flocculent clouds whisper dreams.

. . . thousand, three one thousand, four one thousand . . .

1943

Love, I write you from where I cannot say—
Cannons fire, flash, thunder—My foxhole
Is mud because it just rained—lightning and
Thunder—and stars pass. When will I be home?
Don't ask, because I don't know. I'll never
Forget our wedding day—and that is not
A cliché . . . Don't ask when I will be home
Because there is a war to win and we're
A pawn to victory—Please don't ask when
I'll be home, because I don't know, can't say,
And the stars pass and it hurts not to know.

. . . breathe, one one thousand, two one thousand, three . . .

1994

Under the morning moon, wary fragments
Of mangled lives are glaciers, retreating
North in slow, haunting measures.
Brilliant days,
Somewhere between blue, dirt and sea I seek
Oh Oregon! Mighty glacier, marker
Of cradle and tomb—
Reflections of pure
Sunlight strike the windshield, splinter into
The car—I'm consumed by the morning moon
And disconnected, generative sky.

. . . one thousand, four one thousand, breathe, one one . . .

1993

I've seen too much of hospitals lately—
Wires, alarms, and straps to keep your arms
From flailing about. Your rolling shoulders.

How like a crib is a hospital bed.

Your touch, always gave me headaches.
I grasp your hand, kiss your lips—does it hurt?

. . . three one thousand, four one thousand, breathe.

Envoy

Ashes to ashes, sea to sea, and stars
Pass and billboards tell me where I'm going
For a fee—Oregon! who I only
Saw before in pictures grimy from time
Hands and thoughts—the Columbia River
Empties to the sea, to the Pacific.
Oh say can you see ashes become sea.
Speak now or forever . . . lightning, thunder,
You can ask now—I will hold my peace, Love.

PATRICK KANOUSE, a graduate of Ball State University, lives in Indianapolis where he is an editor with the Macmillan Company.

WALTER R. SMITH

Destinations

A Presbyterian View

THIRTY-THREE YEARS AGO A FRIEND OF MINE DIED because he was a gentleman. He had boarded a plane in New York that would take him back to the University of Miami in Florida. A lame woman got onto the plane and was distressed that there were no seats left. That would mean she would have to go to one of the other three planes flying to Miami, which would be difficult considering her physical handicap. My friend offered his seat to her and got on one of the other planes. On the new flight, a businessman went into the lavatory with his attaché case and exploded a bomb that killed all the travelers on board. Did my friend die because he was a gentleman or was my friend predestined to die? Were the circumstances leading up to my friend's fate coincidental or were they divine intervention? Did he reach the City of God?

PREDESTINATION is one of the most misunderstood and troubling doctrines of Presbyterianism. People assume that predestination means everything in life is predetermined—a way of thinking that leads to fatalism and eliminates all human responsibility. If we do not have some control over the course of our lives, then why should we bother to do anything constructive? However, predestination does not mean life events are predetermined. Is it not possible to come to some understanding of predestination that allows us to see how we fit in God's plan, reaffirms our free participation in that plan, but yet gives God the power to work out God's purpose? I think there is.

A GOOD ILLUSTRATION of this predestination dilemma can be found in the Joseph narratives of the book of Genesis. These narratives comprise over a fourth of the book of Genesis and contain all the ingredients for a best-selling novel: hatred and jealousy among brothers, resentment for parents, attempted murder, slavery, seduction, imprisonment, power, wealth, and the fulfillment of a young, ambitious Jewish man, who despite all odds, rises to be ruler of Egypt, second only to Pharaoh. The only thing that appears to be missing is God.

In the first thirty-six chapters of Genesis, God takes an active role in the creation of the world, and in the lives of the people God calls. It is God who brings forth every living creature, and makes men and women in his own image. God talks intimately with Adam, Eve, Noah, Abraham, Isaac, and Jacob. Covenants are made, wombs are opened, crises are overcome, a rainbow is set in the heavens, children are given in old age, all by a God who walks and talks with his people, and protects them with love and compassion.

This is not the case with the story of Joseph. In chapter thirty-seven God stops talking. God is nowhere to be found. God is alluded to in a few instances, but he doesn't speak again until chapter forty-six when he tells Jacob that he shouldn't be afraid of going to Egypt to live with his son Joseph. Not only is God silent for nine chapters, but when God speaks, it's insignificant in light of the magnitude and the emotion of this story—he only calms the fears of an old man. One can't help but think that the Biblical writers deliberately wrote God out of the script. Why is God so silent? Has God abandoned his people or lost his power? The actors in the Joseph story go about their daily lives as if God didn't matter. Is this a God who is irrelevant—who sets the world in motion, and then turns it over to people to work things out?

Old Testament scholars Gerhard von Rad and Walter Brueggemann believe that the story of Joseph was written in the period of Solomon—the tenth century BCE. During this time, Israel enjoyed a period of prosperity, advancement in knowledge, and competency in the running of everyday affairs of life. Brueggemann says that this period of time is not unlike our own. We too have advancements in knowledge unequaled in the history of the world. The effect of such advancement creates a secular age in which many questions arise about God. When a people have so much knowledge and competency, what does it mean to trust in God? Is God necessary to a world in which human control seems established and sufficient? Do we need God when we have science? This was not a time, Brueggemann says, that questioned the reality or existence of God, but a time when God was treated as irrelevant and unnecessary.[1]

Brueggemann is of the opinion that the writers of Joseph's story deliberately made it a secular story, and gave God what seemed to be an insignificant role. The writers knew that sophisticated people wouldn't listen to such God-talk as found in the first part of Genesis—they would laugh at such foolishness. But the writers also needed to answer the charge that God was irrelevant, lacked power, and that it was humans who made the important choices.[2]

In the story of Joseph, the people go about their everyday tasks unaware, for the most part, of the presence of God, and it should be noted that this human activity is not condemned. The story embraces power, intelligence, knowledge, political activity, shrewdness, and the ability to make decisive decisions for the good of all people. Political power is seen as a way to serve the community faithfully.[3] In addition, Brueggemann says it shows that human activity is the arena of God's action—the place where God's saving work is done.[4] However, it also shows that while God doesn't determine the actions of humans, God can use those actions to accomplish his will. The people in Joseph's story have total freedom in deciding their actions, but so does God.

God is not dependent on human activity to accomplish his purpose, nevertheless God is not free from it either. God works through people. Joseph doesn't reject his brothers, nor does he reject Pharaoh's call to save Egypt. God is not partial to national boundaries—all are God's children. If Joseph had rejected them, the dream would have been destroyed. Because Joseph is faithful to God, God saves two nations.

Joseph is the towering figure in this story, but we must not forget Pharaoh. Even though Pharaoh didn't acknowledge a deity higher than himself, he was smart enough to see Joseph's wisdom, which came from God, and accept Joseph's leadership. Pharaoh opened the door so that God could save Egypt from a great famine, and in that way Pharaoh was faithful to God.

Nor can we forget Joseph's brothers who seemed, at the beginning of the story, to show no respect for God—they attempted to kill their brother and then lied to their father about Joseph's fate. Yet at the end of the story, they seem genuinely changed by the course of events. They acknowledge Joseph's authority by bowing down to him, which, of course, we know signifies that they are bowing to the

---

[1] Walter Brueggemann. *Genesis: A Bible Commentary for Preaching and Teaching.* Atlanta: John Knox Press, 1982. p. 291f; Gerhard von Rad. *Old Testament Theology I.* New York: Harper & Row, 1962. pp. 48–86.

[2] Brueggemann, *Genesis.* pp. 288–298.

[3] Ibid., p. 296.

[4] Ibid., p. 346.

will of God. Joseph did not reject his brothers, and in the end, his brothers did not reject him.

Now we find out what we've suspected all along. It was God's actions—not the brothers'—that brought Joseph to Egypt. God rescued the Hebrews (and the Egyptians) from a universal human catastrophe. It was God—the hidden God—the one who has been silent—the one who hasn't been seen in this story—who worked out his purpose. The dream Joseph had at the beginning of the story was God's dream, and God made it come true. As a result, the Hebrews and the Egyptians are given food by Joseph, God, the real provider.

WITHIN THE WORD PREDESTINATION is the word destiny, and that is exactly what predestination is all about. It is our destiny to reach the City of God that is determined, not the path by which we arrive. Human beings have the freedom to make choices, but they must do so with their destinies in mind. Gertrude Tremblay, a Swedenborgian scholar, puts it this way:

> Predestined to heaven means that a place is maintained for us in the heavens if we want to accept it because that is what God wants for us. We are predestined to heaven not by our choice but by the Lord's constant balancing and re-balancing of the equilibrium between heaven and hell in which we are kept while in this world. God does not create the world and then leave it. God acts behind the scenes without our being aware of it to bring about the results that in his sight are in the best interests of all concerned.[5]

In the story of Joseph, the working out of divine will took place in the normal everyday interaction of life. Little was mentioned of God, yet God's will prevailed. In many respects, predestination is more about the present world than it is about the fulfillment of God's kingdom. To get to the fulfillment, we must first live in the present. The present world is preparing us for the fulfillment of God's kingdom just as living in the womb prepared us for life outside the womb. We could no more leap over our experience in the womb to live without life support, than we can jump over life on earth to get to the fulfillment of the kingdom. What we know is that God will fulfill his kingdom—the future is secured—we don't have to worry about that. What we don't know is when and how we'll get there.

[5] Gertrude Tremblay. Personal communication.

WALTER R. SMITH lives in Lynchburg, Virginia, where he is a minister who enjoys writing. He was born in Hampton, Virginia, raised on Long Island and in Los Angeles. He has been published in Central Virginia Life Magazine and Writer's Report.

Additional Reading and Notes

THERE ARE THREE CLASSICAL WAYS of understanding predestination. The first is associated with John Calvin and is known as Double Predestination. This is the belief that some are chosen to be saved for eternal life and some are damned. The strength of this view is that it shows that God is God and will do what God wants to do. It also explains why some never believe in God. Its weakness is that it is a harsh doctrine that flies in the face of the love and mercy of God, and the theory gives one the impression that all is determined and nothing can be done to change the course of events. In all fairness to Calvin, however, he never made predestination or double predestination a central tenet of his theology. The doctrine never receives systematic treatment in his early writings; he devotes only four chapters to it in his 1559 edition of the *Institutes* (Wendel pp. 264–265), and *that* after he talked about his great themes of freedom, love, grace, and mercy of God and the divinity of Christ. So predestination for Calvin was an extension of God's love. It was the final consequence of faith, not the first act of faith. Therefore, while his writings on the subject seem harsh, Calvin was probably much more lenient than we have thought.

Universalism is another way to look at predestination. It says that all people will be saved—it is God's purpose to save everyone and everyone will be saved—even the most evil people of the world. Its strength is that it shows God's love for all. Its weakness is that it ignores the wrath and judgment of God that indicates that unloving and unbelieving people have no place in the kingdom of God, especially if they continue in their opposition to God.

A third way of understanding predestination is Plegianism, named for the fifth-century British monk Pelagius who first proposed the doctrine. The main point here is that it is all up to you. If you want to be saved, God will save you. God chooses those who choose him. Its strength is that it emphasizes that we have much responsibility for our own salvation. Pelagianism's weakness, however, is that it seemingly makes God powerless and dependent on human decisions.

Bibliography

Guthrie, Jr., Shirley C. *Christian Doctrine.* Atlanta: John Knox Press, 1968. For a further explanation of predestination the reader is referred to pages 125–147, which is chapter seven. This book has recently been revised.

Wendel, Francois. *Calvin: Origins and Development of His Religious Thought.* New York: Harper & Row, 1963.

Warren, Samuel M. A. *Compendium of Swedenborg's Theological Writings.* New York: Swedenborg Foundation, 1977 (first published in 1875).

SYLVIA MONTGOMERY SHAW

Enrique

YEARS AGO WHEN I WAS A CHILD who spent her summers in Mexico, I knew an impish little boy. We called him Quico (key-koh). He was, I learned, named after our great grandfather, Enrique Zepeda, a heroic figure who loomed large in our imagination for having been murdered during the Mexican Revolution. No one ever connected the two Enriques: the doomed man and this child. But I have not stopped thinking of the thread that links them, for I've come to believe it binds us all.

The family albums generously record our presence from the cradle up; my earliest memory of Quico places us at Aunt Julie's wedding, eye-level with an enormous cake. We had decided to inspect it with his brother Pepe. Quico held out his index finger and slid it straight into the white frosting. Pepe and I giggled but didn't dare imitate him. Quico tasted it and went in for a second foray. Just then a man told us to turn around and look into the camera. I tried to look innocent while Pepe hammed it up for the camera and Quico smiled close-lipped to conceal the glob of frosting in his mouth. Then he returned to the cake despite our narrow escape. I remember that he was always taking bold plunges while Pepe and I looked on.

I knew my cousin Enrique back when reality and fantasy merged easily, back when summer days were inhabited by scores of relatives, kings and queens from Narnia, statues that talked, and animals that understood us. Imagination was experience.

Enrique's eyes reflected the world back to me—a world enchanting as our grandfather's garden. It was a time when we could catch dozens of tiny frogs and marvel at their diminutiveness. Across the years I remember our laughter of surprise and delight when the cardboard box slipped out of our hands; scores of frogs escaped into the forbidden: his mother's living room with its delicate brocades and white carpeting.

Enrique and I pledged at six to love each other always, to get married, and to live forever in grandma's house. I made the same promise to Pepe, who outranked us by six months. Protected by twelve-foot walls embroidered with ivy, the three of us explored grandma's garden, played our games and rescued chicks that had fallen from their nests. We wrapped the dead ones in soft folds of tissue, burying them at the foot of the wooden crucifix that our atheist grandfather had placed in the garden—a monument half-hidden, like hope, behind high shrubbery. The carefully pruned bushes formed a sanctuary for the bronze Christ nailed to the cross, hands clenched in agony, knees drawn up, eyes closed in silent suffering. We gazed at him as we buried our tiny dead. The gentle face comforted as much as the tortured body disquieted.

Opposite: Sylvia and Quico in Mexico.

Enrique had beautiful eyes, dark and thick-lashed. Large brown mirrors, they shone through the difficult adolescent years of severe acne, parental divorce, poor grades and eroding self-confidence. Gone was his conviction that we could grow up to be anything we wanted. My spirited cousin had changed like the skies over the capital. A smog-grey sadness gradually settled over Enrique as he failed in school after school. When he dropped out, grandfather came to the rescue with a job in the family firm. Months later Enrique failed there too.

"Your cousin doesn't know anything!" my grandfather told me that summer. "He can't even spell the simplest words! And have you ever seen his handwriting? Chicken scratch."

Years later as I'd struggle to read the "chicken scratch" of some of my students, bright kids with low scores and even lower self-esteem, I would wonder if Enrique was also learning disabled,—unable to read, overlooked, passed on and failed in the end. My grandfather, a self-educated man, glared at my cousin's ill-formed, misspelled words and attributed them to a lazy mind that had wasted opportunity. Grandfather shook his head and gave up on him.

As Pepe and I went on to college, Quico took up the role of playboy. He had long since given up the idea of becoming a veterinarian. He now defined his life in terms of the country club, girl friends, and a red mustang whose horn blared out a ridiculous tune every time he pulled into his driveway. I'd hear it in my deepest sleep across the street in grandma's house. The whole block, nine houses all inhabited by family, would stir and sigh, collectively, "Quico's home." Some found the horn irritating. But for most of us it was part of our nocturnal landscape, a sound comforting in its familiarity. It was Quico's greeting to the family—loud, brief and exuberant.

When I married a Yankee from Massachusetts, my Mexican summers dwindled to one or two-week visits every few years. I saw my cousin Enrique, briefly, usually at family weddings. But I would hear that ridiculous horn in the middle of the night and smile. The beautiful little boy who had stumbled through awkward adolescence, had grown into full adulthood: tall, bearded, and handsome. A quiet man with a quiet sense of humor, he knew how to laugh at himself.

"Do you remember the time you helped me save face with Ethquenathi?" he asked me as we danced at a cousin's wedding.

"Esquenazi?"

All his life Enrique spoke with a slight lisp that altered "s" to "th." We all loved it. It gave a charming Castilian lilt to his Spanish.

I thought back to our adolescence and remembered the first time I met his buddy, "Ethquenathi." Enrique had whispered to me, "Please don't let on you're my cousin!" He then introduced me as his girl friend. Seeing the triumph on his face, I squeezed his hand. Years later Enrique laughed as he told me about his boast to Esquenazi that he could get himself an American girl friend within a week. The friend had sworn the same.

"It turns out Esquenazi had American cousins too," he smiled.

Enrique was a charmer. But when he finally settled down and married a lovely girl from Northern Mexico, he floundered from one failed enterprise to another. Only two of his efforts came to fruition: his children, two boys with big brown eyes. Ultimately he failed them too.

Enrique and I met again one luminous morning in Cuernavaca, a resort town near Mexico City. He had moved in with his father after he and his wife separated. We sat by a pool shaded by jacaranda trees. Lavender blossoms floated on the water. My little Gabe and Alex splashed about trying to scoop up the flowers. Enrique watched them. I could sense he was missing his own children.

"You have nice kids," he told me.

"I'm told you do too. Do you get to see them?"

"Not much. Mali moved back with her parents." He turned and looked directly into my face for the first time in our conversation. "You look happy with your life."

It was a statement of fact without envy. For a few seconds I saw the little boy in those dark eyes.

"I am. I hope things work out for you too, Quico."

He seemed tired, but he still believed he would succeed in his newest business venture and recoup his marriage. Time passed.

When I next heard about Enrique, I was pregnant with my third child. On a particularly vibrant morning, the kind drenched with sunlight and infused with the conviction that all is right with the world, we received a phone call. My mother asked Holland, my husband, to break the news to me carefully. He in turn told me the truth the only way he knows how: directly.

"It's bad news from Mexico, so I'm going to tell you outright. Your cousin Quico is dead. He's been murdered."

Murdered. . . .

I pictured a thief; a gun shot; running feet.

"What do you mean, murdered? Tell me."

"He was arrested by the Cuernavaca police on trumped-up charges . . . and was tortured to death. I'm sorry," Holland murmured gently.

I insisted on the details, sketchy as they were at that point. As I grappled with seeing and not seeing in my mind what they had done to him, as the story of my uncle's search for his son unfolded across the miles, as I cried desolately for my poor cousin, I did one more thing: I blocked out all memory of him as an adult. I found over the next weeks as my body grew, that I could only remember Quico as a little boy. No matter how hard I strained to remember the adult face, I could no longer bring it to mind. I had in effect locked my cousin into childhood where he could be safe.

I WAKE UP THINKING I AM IN MY OLD ROOM at grandma's, and Quico is blowing that absurd horn. But the air is chilled and the night too quiet and my body too awkward. I struggle out of bed and grope for my slippers. My body tells me I'm thirty seven, and nine months pregnant. This is now, not then, and it is winter in all its cold indifference.

I drape a comforter over my shoulders and walk softly to the window. Silence. Such silence. The baby inside me lies still as the night. I flick on the flood lights and discover a flurry of activity. It's snowing, and I know how far I am from Mexico. December. I'm full term now, reading, but my thoughts have returned to Enriqué, to a room I can only imagine, to a night protracted and distorted by pain and terror.

If my husband were to wake up just now and see me by the window, he would come over, wrap his arms around my shoulders, murmur into my hair, "Don't dwell on it. It's over now." My agnostic husband might even remind me about heaven and that Quico is at peace now. And then I would have to tell Holland what I'm thinking tonight as snow buries us: that heaven isn't enough; that believing in a life after death doesn't take away the horror of what they did to Enrique: that I'm scared because for all my faith in the high purpose of human life, I can't find my way past terror into transcendence.

I try once again to remember my cousin as a man, refusing to hunt for him in the scrapbooks, determined to retrieve him by my own powers. Only a smooth-faced child approaches through the storm. I remember Insurgentes Avenue, choked with traffic. A poor street dog is hit by the car in front of us. I watch the silent snow and hear Quico's sharp cries of anguish as he begs my aunt: "Poor little dog! We've got to help him!" The dog's shrill yelps and the boy's anguish rush together in the silent room, and I remember that those men beat Enrique with crowbars, that they branded and castrated him. A woman who was being beaten in the next room and who survived the ordeal told the family that Enrique kept begging his torturers to name their price, that he would pay them anything. Only stop! He kept begging. Please stop!

And the woman sobs as she tells the family. A dog yelps in a frenzy of pain; a boy wrings his hands in anguish, a man screams in terror and I hear them all and cry into the peaceful night because there is no peace, no rest, no compassion. Only pain. And though I pull myself together for the sake of my husband and children and unborn child, though I return to my days with cheeriness and energy, I am torn inside, and I go into labor carrying all those cries inside me.

I am in intensive labor. My mother is with me. My husband. My doctor, an intern, and two nurses. The doctor, who had promised me anesthesia if I changed my mind about a natural delivery, deliberately withholds all medication from me. I see the nurse holding the syringe. She glances uneasily at me and at the doctor; he waves her away. I beg for the injection. She hesitates. Again, he motions with his hands. No. And I see another room, as real as this one, with dark faces. Men in uniform, leering at me, laughing at my agony. They are real. They are there, dark-faced strangers. And I am Enrique. I am Enrique and there is only terror and pain. Brutality.

Later, when it is all over and the doctor stitches me without the usual xylocaine to numb the pain, later when I moan, "How many more stitches?" He jokes, "Oh . . . about a hundred!" and he boasts to his student, "Yep! This is as natural a delivery as you'll ever see!" Even then, as I realize I have been used as a lesson and that my pain was immaterial, my mind races back to that moment when the ordeal reached its climax. I return to that moment just before the baby's birth when I felt so alone despite those around me. With eyes shut tight, disembodied, no longer a woman giving birth but a man tortured with branding irons and blades, I see somewhere in that overlapping of realities a window.

It hangs suspended in a white wall. A window floating on a wall or in a sky. Disembodied like me. The frenzied pain stops. The people vanish. A fierce wind blows through the room. Shutters slam open with a tremendous thud and I gasp, elated, awe-struck:

"He's born!"

Not my child who has entered the world at that very moment, but Enrique who has slipped through their hands; Enrique: no longer afraid; untouchable. Like me, he feels relief. Surprise. Wonder.

SYLVIA MONTGOMERY SHAW is a high school teacher and writer who lives in Massachusetts. She says: "It has been eight and a half years since that afternoon in the delivery room. I am often reminded as I gaze into the vibrant face of my son, Daniel, that there is no more vivid a metaphor for pain and transcendence than labor and delivery. All pain is finite; it has its allotted time. But we must never turn a blind eye to human rights violations that occur daily around the world. Every victim is someone's Enrique."

ANN GRABER WESTERMANN

Into the Spiral and Out

ALTHOUGH I HAD BELIEVED IN A REALITY beyond the tangible world since childhood, it was largely a matter of faith. Faith became knowing on September 10, 1984, when a gateway to another dimension or plane of awareness flew open for me. On that day my life changed dramatically, both inwardly and outwardly.

On a vacation trip a year earlier I had been involved in an automobile accident. The rear-end collision resulted in an undetected injury to my neck, which caused discomfort and increasing numbness of my left arm and hand. I found I could relieve the pain and pressure in my neck by dangling my head over the edge of the bed before going to work. This is what I was doing on that fateful morning when I slid off the bed and landed on the back of my neck. As my body hit the floor, I felt an excruciating pain—as if my spinal cord had been cut by a knife—followed by a lightening-like sensation surging down my spine and exiting through every nerve ending; then nothing, no sensation, no movement! I lay crumpled on the floor the way I had fallen and could not move. A horrible realization dawned on me: I am paralyzed!

Following the shock of the impact of this discovery, I began to assess my situation. As a former anatomy/physiology instructor, I concluded that I had sustained a traumatic spinal cord injury with loss of function and sensation below the neck and was quadriplegic. Since I could still breathe unassisted, I deduced that the lesion must be below C-3 (the third cervical vertebra).

I was fully conscious and painfully aware of my predicament. This fall happened around 7:30 AM on a Monday morning. Everyone in the house had already left for the day. I was alone. No one was expected to be back before evening. My thoughts and feelings reacted with voices of their own: Will I still be alive by then? It didn't matter; I was a quad. Given our current level of medical technology, we simply didn't know how to mend mangled spinal cords. Who wants to live in a body that doesn't function? And, my worst fear of all: What if I was comatose and could not object to being kept alive through mechanical means? The horror of that possibility engulfed me. An intense rush of self-pity overwhelmed me.

Then some aspect from deep within stepped forth and took charge as if to say, "Stop your snivelling! You can't wipe your nose; you can't raise your head; you will choke. This is not the time to feel sorry for yourself. Use what little time you have left to put your inner house in order." It was as if the CEO of my intrapsychic board of regents had spoken. This appeared to be a sensible suggestion. I was surprised to learn that the emotions did not have to run the show, that a higher wisdom could be in charge. Heeding its directive I had to conclude that I was probably about to die. How does one prepare to die—consciously? Not someday when I'm old, but now, perhaps in a matter of hours.

As my bodily functions and sensations diminished, perceptions became keener. Never before or since have I been able to think so clearly and rapidly. It seemed as if my central nervous system were an organ through which mind operated in the physical plane. As the veil of matter was lifting I had direct access to mind, unencumbered by limiting neural pathways. I perceived myself more and more from outside of my body confines. It felt as if my life force was being withdrawn through the crown of my head and was gathering above me.

This process took several hours. I became the observer and the observed. For instance, I could dispassionately observe that the circulation was cut off in my left leg (I had landed in a heap with my weight compressing the left leg). I watched it turn pale and then waxen-looking as if it belonged to a corpse. At the same time I felt deep sadness for it, boundless gratitude for having carried me through life, and the joy of dancing and skiing on it. In this expanded state of awareness everything was happening simultaneously with great intensity. It was a transtemporal experience: I was in linear time as well as beyond it.

The thought occurred to me to do a "general confession with an act of contrition" as I had been taught in my Catholic childhood: to ask for forgiveness wherever I knew I had wronged someone and to extend mine where I harbored resentment. As soon as I had that intention clearly formulated, my memory banks opened up as never before. Suddenly I had access to past experiences in a multisensory way. I not only saw the events of my life pass before me, but sensed the wider implications of every act in a holographic progression. I was acutely aware of how I and others felt at the same time. I knew, for example, each and every child in my third-grade class again. I could clearly see the wispy pigtails of the little girl in front of me; my attention was drawn to the intricate Norwegian design of a boy's sweater; I was hearing the teacher's voice and knowing what impact he had made on each of us—far beyond the lessons we had studied in class. And so it went through the many days and years of my life. I was amazed at the mental acuity at my disposal. Everything I had ever learned was stored knowledge available to me, in glorious color with surround sound, complete with smells and tastes, accompanied by feelings. It was incredible! A holodome of my personal journey.

When I reached the end of my life review, a dizzying perceptual ride through more than four decades, I felt great relief. I saw it as a life rich in meaningful experiences; some happy, some painful, but an eventful life with many challenges and opportunities for soul growth. There were some unhealed relationships into which I poured all my love and good will, trusting that the force of my intention would carry my message of reconciliation to its destination.

Then I began to say my goodbyes. With deep love and caring I took my leave from those near and dear to me. As the circle of love expanded, I was amazed to see how many people had influenced my life and had made a contribution to my growth. I began to understand how interconnected we all are. At that moment it was easy to love the whole world and everybody in it. Gradually I reached a point of relinquishment where I concluded—it was a good life! If I had to do it over, I probably wouldn't do any better. This was very comforting. A tranquility and stillness began to permeate my entire being. I was at peace. All fear of death had vanished. The sun was high on the horizon now. My breathing was shallow and very labored. Death would be a welcome visitor. My last conscious thought was, "Into your hands I commend my spirit, Oh Lord!"

What I am about to relate next needs to be prefaced. No one says it better than Emanuel Swedenborg when he tells of spirit slipping into a stillness at death, rather like falling asleep, and experiencing inexpressible Divine things of infinite wisdom; of seeing countless things, of which not even a ten/thousandth part could be described in human words because they would not fit into concepts that have matter-centered content (*Heaven and Hell,* paragraph no. 411).

After having surrendered my life into God's keeping, the scene shifted. Awareness of the room where I had lain on the floor faded. I was somewhere else! Trying to orient myself to my new surroundings, I found myself in space somewhere. In the distance I could see our beautiful planet, the Earth, glistening and turning gracefully. I sensed that I was not alone. There were presences about me, very benevolent essences. I did not perceive them as having form, but they were identifiable by their inner qualities, which radiated from them and permeated this realm, giving it a shimmering purplish-golden glow. It was a wondrous place or state of being. I was on hallowed ground and my soul was having a sacred encounter. My impression was of swirling currents of unimaginable intelligence filled with compassion, radiant love, infinite wisdom, aliveness and vitality that sustained worlds without end. These qualities were as palpable as tangible objects are in our world, not abstract or elusive. I was wondrously safe there. I was home.

Isabel Bishop. *Nude.* Tempera on gesso panel, 20¾×17¾ inches, ca. 1938. Tucson: The University of Arizona Museum of Art. Gift of C. Leonard Pfeiffer.

I felt warmly welcomed and was given to understand that my life task was accomplished. The thought of spending eternity here filled me with ecstasy. Then a drama was staged for my education and benefit. Our Earth was shown to me. It had points of light as well as places of darkness. There were many changes occurring rapidly all around it. This appeared to me as energy vortices twirling, picking up momentum, colliding with others, changing direction and velocity, regrouping and reforming, gradually learning to cooperate for the benefit of all; until eventually they moved with grace and beauty in harmony with one another. The implication was: there is and will be much chaotic whirling of energies about the planet Earth. There is need for souls there who can be stable elements, points of stillness, while the winds of change and transformation blow about. I intuited an invitation, "Will you be one of them?"

What? Go back into that crumpled body that's beyond repair? I didn't want to leave this wondrous golden-purple realm, nor the company of those magnificent beings! But I gave my consent to return and immediately I became conscious of being on the floor in my room. The door was being opened. Against all odds, someone came by at noon and found me. I was taken to a hospital that specialized in treating neurological injuries. After many months in traction, a spinal fusion, rehabilitation, the ministrations of many kinds of healers, the loving support of kindred spirits, my recovery exceeded the most optimistic medical prognosis.

Has looking through that window beyond finite consciousness made a difference in my life? The first and most immediate change was in my attitude regarding death. If I believed in a life after death before, now I know that consciousness lives on. Moreover, I had experienced the transition from three-dimensional to multi-dimensional reality; it is an adventure to be looked forward to, not an event to be feared.

I also live with a greater sense of purpose, knowing that each of us has a vocation of destiny or life purpose: to do that which is most meaningful for us to do at a given time and circumstance. Life is a gift, not a given. We are to respond to the demands life places upon us, meet its challenges, by utilizing our innate resources. We have a mandate to become all that we can be. We each play a part in the symphony of life. The orchestra of planet Earth is practicing its hymn to the universe. There may still be discordant notes to be heard, but we are getting more attuned to each other and to the conductor. It will be a glorious sound when everyone knows their part.

My own part in the symphony of life has undergone drastic changes since that life-transforming event. There was an inner mandate to reevaluate priorities, which led me through career as well as lifestyle changes. Living meaningfully and making a qualitative difference became my endeavor. As a direct result of my remarkable experience I wanted to assist others who are facing serious crises in their lives, especially those dealing with the fear of dying. To that end I sought ordination as an interfaith minister, pledged to serve the spiritual needs of all seekers.

I also studied and became credentialed in logotherapy, the meaning-centered psychotherapy and philosophy founded by Viktor Frankl, the Viennese psychiatrist. His therapeutic approach provides the tools I need for facilitating the desired transformation. Frankl's emphasis on the noetic core as a source of healing and self-transcendence matches my own experience and belief.

In my personal life, relationships underwent transitions. My marriage of many years, as well as some friendships that had held great meaning for me, were no longer sustainable. I mourned those losses deeply. But other people appeared on my path who accepted me and were eager to know about experiences beyond finite consciousness. Doors have been opening and opportunities to be of service abound.

Direct experience of the sacred is our birthright. Since that glimpse into another dimension, there has indeed been much swirling of energies about the planet. By and large, awareness is shifting and our concepts of reality are expanding with increasing rapidity, predisposing us for a reunion with the sacred. As more and more of us access that greater reality within, fear will lessen; not only the fear of death, but also the fear of each other, and bridges of trust will be built to facilitate harmonious interactions. Experiences beyond finite consciousness are not the purview of a select few, but the common destiny and heritage of humankind.

ANN GRABER WESTERMANN, M.DIV., Diplomate of the Viktor Frankl Institute of Logotherapy, lives and works in Missouri. She is the author of an audiotape album, *Images of Transformation.*

BESS WILCOXON

The Soap

The shower sprays
A forgotten perfume.
I am holding the new soap
Pretending it is raining.
Soap mist is rising
But not of the new soap;
It is the scent of the old soap.
Summer foliage
Arbors the tub enclosure.
Simple flowers
Lean out of the old garden.
Suddenly my children
Rise about me playing.
They are small again.
They ring my Eve body,
And the rain shower flows
Over their faces.
They circle beneath my arms
Laughing and whirling.
Their faces flash past
Wearing each of their ages,
That many times
Until almost twenty.
I gasp with love
For their changing faces.
In the scent of the soap,
I shower endlessly.
The new soap, the old soap
Washes and washes.

BESS WILCOXON, a retired English teacher in Hampton, Virginia, says she has been a poet, although unpublished, all of her life.

PART IV

Earth, Sky, Transformation

NINA ROMANO

Angel of the Lord

WHEN HEROD THE GREAT was tetrarch of Galilee and Jesus Christ was about two years old, I was six. I wore a loose white garment and sienna sandals. It was hot. Wherever I went, there was dust and sand. I walked swiftly because someone was following me and there were shadows everywhere. Long shadows thrown against the walls of outer buildings that appeared to be a small village complex. I never returned there, but I would recognize it instantly were I ever to see it again.

The Archangel Gabriel. Workshop of Dionisy, ca. 1502. Leningrad: The Russian Museum.

I began to run. I was afraid. My hands clenched and my stomach quivered like the feathers on a badly released arrow. Only upon entering the atrium of a clay home that had no windows, no doors, did I feel at all comfortable. My pace slowed a bit. Moving quickly through what appeared to be a maze of many twists and turns, I found myself on my way to yet another home. Once inside, I discovered that before I could rest or gulp a breath of air I had already reached outside again. Crouching in a courtyard, I still looked for refuge because I was afraid and knew I was hunted. Although I couldn't fathom why the search had been sanctioned and by whom, I kept running from house to house, trying to hide.

I realized who was chasing me, though, when I turned to look over my shoulder. It shocked me to recognize the short tunic and helmet of Roman soldiers approaching, the hilts of their drawn swords in their hands and light glinting from the blades. It seemed that I was just steps ahead of them as I darted from room to room. Luckily, I spied a tall rush basket in an unused alcove. I tried to jump into the basket, but my legs were too short. The wicker receptacle overturned, and the bolts of muted colored cottons contained within the basket fell.

A man pushed the lid aside, righted the basket and helped me in. The strangest feeling of no feeling, like the touch of an eyelash on skin, prevailed as he lifted a smaller, lighter me and placed me gently in the deep plaited container. Aware of his presence, I never remember actually seeing him while he arranged some loose cloths about my head to cover and hide me. As it became darker due to the covering, I sensed him tossing the cloths about, like someone making a salad, and I supposed it was to help me breathe more easily. It became even darker when he covered the basket with the lid.

Yet I could peer out through the woven reeds. I saw thick breastplates; short, pleated skirts; leather thongs crisscrossed around the muscular legs of soldiers. I heard weeping as soldiers sought out other hidden children. My fear became intense, but a great light streamed through the interlacings and I knew my hiding place was secure. Shouts in words I didn't comprehend became fainter as the shuffling of Roman sandaled feet explored the dwelling. Noises and scents of overturned wine carafes, jars of oil, and incense in a distant part of the abode diminished. A great hush descended—like the stars settling into the night sky.

Then everything was quiet, calm, and bright. I had a sense of weightlessness and knew in that instant the soldiers were gone and I was safe and at peace. My eyelids fluttered, my cheeks cooled, and I felt relieved because I was still alive.

When I opened my eyes, my mother was sitting by my side on my maple four-poster bed, stroking my hair. I told her what happened to me and she said I had been dreaming because I was very sick with a high fever.

I said, "Oh, no, I wasn't dreaming. I was there."

From that day to this I can still see myself, the soldiers, the houses, the light. I can feel the warmth, the gritty dust of parched earth, the fear; and know what I lived through was not a dream, but a frame in time, caught as a memory that I will have with me always.

NINA ROMANO received a bachelor's degree from Ithaca College and a master's degree from Adelphi University. After residing in Rome for twenty years, where she acquired fluency in Italian and Spanish, she returned to the United States and is now working on a master's degree in the fine arts.

PATTI TANA

Last Morning in Jerusalem

The hotel faces the Old City
where my son feels at home
among the stones and trees.

Which ones did my pennies plant
from the blue tin cans of youth,
each one placed by other hands?

Light rain burnishes
the pink and golden stones,
freshens the parched earth.

Turning from the window, I pack
the kiddish cup, replicas of Miriam and Moses,
the moss green stones from Eilat—

richer and poorer for leaving.
Jerusalem, I give you my son.

PATTI TANA is professor of English at Nassau Community College (SUNY) in Garden City, New York. Her most recent book of poems and stories is *Wetlands*.

EDWARD R. BOSLEY

Light: The Natural and the New

As Seen in Greene & Greene's Turn-of-the-Century Architecture

The purpose of using glass in architecture is essentially to have light embrace one's life. It is light that defines one's experience of space; it is light that articulates volume and texture; it is light that marks the passage of the day and reconnects one to nature.

Beyond the simple notion of the passage of light through glass is the more complex idea of modulating or controlling this light through various means. Historically, these can be as diverse as the Roman use of finely sliced sheets of onyx or quartz which would glow with the warmth and pattern of these translucent stones to the wondrously intricate use of stained glass in medieval cathedrals, where the narrative of the parable is projected into the space through light, thereby imbuing the interior with myth.

In our day-to-day lives, the exploration of the transparent boundary that separates interior from exterior (the individual from the world beyond), remains one of the greatest challenges for architects. To make sense of light, to unlock and celebrate its diverse properties of reflection, transmission, and refraction through the glass membrane, is a means to focus our attention and re-engage us with the phenomenon of light and the natural world.

—JAMES CARPENTER

Morning light brings a California oak tree design to life in leaded art-glass. Entry doors, the Gamble House, architects Charles and Henry Greene, 1908.

AS IT GATHERED MOMENTUM in the American home just before the turn of the century, electric-light technology was greeted with high anticipation and hopes that life could be brightened—literally and figuratively—by the filament bulb. Excitement surrounding the potentially convenient domestic uses of the light bulb was suffused, however, with subtle suspicions that the new light might not be all good. Might it eclipse other familiar forms of illumination beyond the seemingly doomed gas lamp? Would electricity limit the role of sunlight in our homes? Thanks to bright electric streetlights, would moonlit strolls become obsolete? Other questions arose about the safety of electricity. There were not only the clear moral issues raised by the potential cruelty of a new form of capital punishment, but the safety of electricity in the home was also at the center of the debate surrounding the first electric chair execution on August 6, 1890. As these emotion-charged issues were addressed over the next decade, the practical advantages of electricity over gas for domestic lighting became clearer, and the safety issue waned, but the sheer esthetic possibilities within the realm of the electric light were as yet not fully developed.

Louis Comfort Tiffany was the most notable American figure to explore the early artistic potential of the electric light. His famous offerings of leaded, art-glass lamps released an unsuspected beauty from the standard, dim filament bulb, the equivalent of about sixteen watts. Tiffany raised the standard of art-glass manufacturing and design to a new, higher level to which architects and designers responded by rethinking the rich creative potential of glass as a lens for artificial and natural lighting. Arts and Crafts architects Charles and Henry Greene (1868–1957 and 1870–1954), whose careers matured concomitantly with the general acceptance of the electric light, designed some of the most spectacular examples of architectural art-glass ever executed for the home, sympathetically joining the practical demands of house design with a personal philosophy of allowing nature, and the nature of materials, to guide esthetic considerations. The resulting designs, mainly of Tiffany-style art-glass, present both artificial and natural lighting as key components of their architectural language. In particular the Gamble house, the Greenes' design for Procter & Gamble Company heirs David and Mary Gamble in Pasadena (1908), brings to a new pinnacle the use of art-glass as an architectural means of reflecting nature.

The Gamble House entry doors and transom lights, designed by Charles Greene and crafted by Emil Lange, express the stately, spreading California oak as a flat-pattern illustration referencing nearby specimens in the Arroyo Seco. Eastern morning light flows directly through the leaded art-glass tree to play yellow, green, and golden hues on the interior paneling and floors. Its branches spanning eleven feet, the entry door oak tree symbolizes the ongoing, postharvest life of wood, the predominant building material in the house. At the far end of the hall opposite the entry doors, a pair of transparent glass doors open to the west terrace, across which, late in the day at certain times of the year, light passes to penetrate the length of the hallway, illuminating the entry doors from behind and giving the lucky passer-by on the street a brief notion of its fully lighted glory. The same afternoon sun passes through the garden and enters the living room through broad panes of clear plate glass. Sunlight hangs mid-air, sheetlike, brightening the reading areas and casting shadows in teak-paneled corners. On the library table a Tiffany-designed lamp, brought by the Gambles from their Cincinnati house, represents the flow of electricity that to them had come to be considered a reliable asset. The lamp's art-glass shade is equipped with a quaint, protective shield—an adjustable butterfly-design panel hanging on a chain from the finial—giving eye protection from the possible dangers of direct exposure to an electric bulb. Close by, a broad inglenook with two reading benches flanks the wide fireplace, itself a window on nature when it crackled behind the inglenook. Each inglenook bench is lighted by its own overhead electric bulb encased in an exquisitely designed fixture, a delicate, pagodalike mahogany and ebony structure. These are suspended by leather straps from a robust teak truss and fitted with iridescent panels of art-glass, leaded and colored to suggest a stylized vine and blossom design as another introduction of nature to the interior. Complex and delicate reflections of the natural world, these fixtures reveal the reverence attached to the presentation of both artificial and natural light by the architects who designed them and by the clients who paid for them.

For the Greenes, a beautiful result was the final goal in resolving any design challenge, but the challenge was often driven by practicality. Thus art-glass was the ideal material for the entry doors: it is translucent to admit light yet opaque enough to obscure the view of the street. Still, not presuming to improve on nature, the architects specified clear windows and doors on the west to admit light and give desirable views toward the garden and terraces. In the dining room, over the massive built-in sideboard, art-glass windows—iridized, leaded, and stained to depict a tea-rose vine—mitigate the close proximity of the neighbors' house to the south.

Across the ages, windows and doors have easily borrowed light and promoted air circulation. But in the hands of Greene & Greene, even these basic tasks were accomplished with great clarity of purpose in the search for beauty in architectural design. The clear window became a frame for nature and a reflector of the architect's and client's priorities for beauty in the home environment. The stained and leaded-glass panel achieved its customary colorful beauty derived from centuries of development, but also became integrated with the working architecture of doors, windows, and the new electric light to harmonize with, not challenge, the natural landscape.

Sadly, home design since the early decades of the century has retreated from what are now considered to be sentimental associations with nature. Is this because we think we understand nature well enough? We now wrap electric lightbulbs in minimalist utilitarian globes, if in anything at all. Why? And what of the moonlit stroll?

EDWARD R. BOSLEY is director of The Gamble House, a National Landmark and the most complete and best preserved work of architects Charles and Henry Greene. Ted holds a bachelor's degree in art history from Berkeley and a master's degree from U.C.L.A. He attributes his initial interest in architecture to the early imprint of that icon of Arts and Crafts esthetics, the Swedenborgian Church in San Francisco, where he has been a member since the age of three. JAMES CARPENTER is principal of James Carpenter Design Associates in New York City. James's work concentrates on the use of glass and daylighting principles in collaboration with architects internationally. A graduate of the Rhode Island School of Design, he has received numerous awards, including the Loeb fellowship at Harvard University.

JOHN L. HITCHCOCK

The Window onto Eternity

WE LIVE IN TWO WORLDS AT ONCE. We might call them the visible world and the "other side." For most of us, the area of experience of which we are most concretely aware is the visible world, the world of our rational consciousness, about which we feel we can make definite statements. We also have abundant *connection* with the "other side," but the contact is usually unconscious. When that contact enters our awareness, we say that there has been an opening of the "window onto eternity," known also by its Latin name, *fenestra aeternitatis.* Though the opening of this window is the stuff of mystical experience, it is, or can be, a staple of everyday living. The window onto eternity is part of the essential structure of our own depths.

This article will give a modern account of the *fenestra aeternitatis* and apply it to examples of some of these openings of our awareness. By "modern," I mean that I intend to account for what happens in terms that are as complete, accurate, and nonsectarian as I can make them. This account will draw upon C.G. Jung's depth psychology through one of its foremost exponents, Erich Neumann, in *The Place of Creation.*[1]

I use the term "other side" to denote a form of experience which is not limited to our "inner being," though our awareness of it usually begins to open for us as we begin to become aware of the structure of our own inwardness. That is, the polarity with which we are concerned is not so much that of inner versus outer as it is of the world of images and concepts versus the formless and eternal *field*

[1] Erich Neumann. *The Place of Creation.* Translated by Hildegard Nagel, Eugene Rolfe, Jan van Heurck, and Krishna Winston. Princeton University Press, 1989.

which gives rise to all visible forms, and is also the source of all dynamism (energy): physical, psychic, and spiritual.

We will look at a few "extraordinary" events in order to see what is *meant* by the window onto eternity. In the end, however, we will be able to see that the window *embraces and encompasses* us at all times—that we are connected *at our core* with everything that seems to be other than ourselves, including life, the Earth, stars, and galaxies, reaching to the limits of the cosmos. In the end, the very distinction of inner and outer is only a relative reality.

WE CANNOT UNDERSTAND the *fenestra aeternitatis* unless we first understand that the "outer world" is a *relative* thing. That is, the *images* that we possess as to what that outer world is like come partly from within ourselves. They do represent definite effects of a concrete and relatively objective outer world, but they do so only partially.

An analogy from the more spiritual side may help give the idea. Where a Christian might have a vision of Christ, a Hindu would have a vision of Krishna, and a Jewish person would have a vision of Elijah. This is a frequent phenomenon of the near-death experience. The two visions have common elements and differences. Both are probably experiences of the same aspect of the "other side," known in near-death parlance as the "being of light," but the experience comes in terms of what is already "known" to the person. The numinous source of both visions remains relatively unknown. The point is that the identity of the figure is determined by the psyche of the one having the vision.

Our scientific images or concepts of physical reality also retain something of the same quality of projection of "known," or assumed, qualities onto the unknown, although to a lesser extent than with the near-death example. Even scientists see things in the first way in which they can grasp them at all, and then tend to say (mistakenly) that this is how things really are. It takes generations of exploration to refine our images of physical reality, and it really is an endless process.

In the formation of a concept of the "external world" we have given it a name and an assumed form. Because this form is always merely provisional, *physical reality itself retains the freedom to give us a surprise at a later time,* and this is indeed the main theme in the history of science. Something new can come through the "window onto eternity," even (or perhaps especially) where we thought we understood things.

Our Inner Mirror

When we form an image of something, we do so by means of contrasts. What we are aware of as the ordinary mental/visual tendency to form figure/ground relationships, actually goes much deeper than the visual recognition process. Our model of consciousness-building *as such* is *becoming aware of opposites, or of contradictions.* One set of opposites, of which we only gradually become aware, is the pair, outer/inner, with which we are concerned in relation to the *fenestra aeternitatis.* A closely related set is the pair "I"/"not-I."

Ego-consciousness, the form of knowledge we have been describing, is a kind of self-reflexivity, which means that it is first of all an abiding mystery, because we are trying to understand "from within." We cannot see things from the outside, for *there is no outside.* This situation applies even to our simplest observation of, say, a pebble. The ego complex, the referent for the field of things of which we are, or can be, conscious, is our organ of self-reflexivity, the mysterious means of our becoming aware of the opposites inherent in the field and in the patterning of the universe. The word *consciousness* consists of the root words for "knowing" and "together," the combination pointing to a sort of passing something back and forth. Self-reflexivity means almost the same thing, and is clearly a more complex kind of thing than what we think of the awareness of lower animals, which does not involve self-questioning.

We can never come to a direct understanding from within, and thus need a sort of "mirror," as in the image of self-reflexivity itself. It is not easy to picture this process. Jung speaks of something in the field, an "obstacle," by means of which *the opposites that the field contains begin to "rub and jostle" each other*; that is, they begin to conflict with each other around the edges of our consciousness.[2] This is a very helpful metaphor, for ordinary reflection occurs by means of an obstacle to the light. All that we see, we see by means of reflected light. In the case of the psyche, however, we don't know what this obstacle, this ego-complex, really is. The best we can say is that it is something like the cosmos becoming aware of itself, in these tiny points within itself, namely us. That is, *we are not separate from the whole.* When the window onto eternity opens for any individual, that person becomes aware of being part of that whole, and sees that ordinary life, which feels disconnected, is an illusion.

In the case of self-reflexivity, something is reflected because the psyche, living in the field, becomes an obstacle to the flow of energy. This applies not only to specific visual images with contrasts, but also

[2] C.G. Jung. *Collected Works.* Translated by R.F.C. Hull. Princeton University Press, 1969. Answer to Job. In *Psychology and Religion: West and East. Collected Works 11.*

to *contradictions* in the way we look at things, which are present because the separation of the two worlds is not the ultimate truth.

Building "Our Own" World

Our mind is well-known for "filling in" missing parts of images to create a *gestalt,* or image of a whole. In this way, we have, through discovering and imaging the *physical* order within the total numinous reality, *constructed* a world-image which has, in effect, driven demons and daimonic powers back into darkness. We have created a world of light which now effectively hides the other side from our consciousness. It is so bright, so powerful a reflection, that it blinds us to more subtle things. The contrasts we have created in constructing a scientific worldview have gradually *closed our interior perception*—closed, in other words, the window onto eternity, which was open more fully before the advent of ego-consciousness. When the mind is able to make contrasts, and those contrasts are mistaken for all that there is, it then seems that the things of the spirit are unreal. It is where we become *aware* of the field and its numinosity that we speak of the opening of the *fenestra aeternitatis.* Through the window, the field connects to, or impacts, our conscious minds.

Of course, we construct much more than the external world; we also construct philosophy, law, ethics, ideologies, and religion. I have left art out of this list, for it is the remaining field where the *fenestra aeternitatis* is relatively open, and inspiration can function to a degree.

The distinction between *inner and outer* reflects only the point of view of *ego-consciousness;* it is just one of the *contrasts* that we have "created" in order to grasp things. We do, however, possess other kinds of knowing for which the distinction between inner and outer does not hold true. That is not to say that the inner/outer distinction is not "real," but the fact is that the other kinds of experience are also real, and the final weight cannot be assigned solely and arbitrarily to the point of view of ego-consciousness.

Ego-consciousness, and the loss of noncontrast awareness, has arisen as we have attempted to separate what is "I" from what is "not-I" in an *external* sense. That is, as we bump into, or discover, things in the "external world," we are also drawn to these outer phenomena and try to understand them. As infants and toddlers, we gradually learn what is our own body, and what is "other" to us in a bodily sense. This develops awareness of differences, of contrasts. There is fascinating consistency and stability to this world, which ends up as the subject matter of physical science. Our understanding, however, is always partial, always drawing upon prior experience to form categories through which to classify what is discovered.

Ego-consciousness turns naturally toward the outer world, because that world is the reality that brought the ego into being, and the world to which the ego is therefore naturally attuned. Of course, it is not only the world of external physical reality, but the place of other persons as well. However, it takes us much longer—usually well into the second half of life—to learn what is "I" and "not-I" with respect to other persons. That is, we very often mistake what is a part of our own inner being as characteristic of, or belonging to, someone outside ourselves. Psychologically, this phenomenon is known as "projection." When we realize our projections, we begin to become aware of our own inner dimension, and its connection to the other side.

In fact, what we experience as inner is experienced by the pre-modern psyche as outer. It is only with the development of the ego that the outer world is divested of spirit, and the latter spirit forced inside and out of sight, as it were. Neumann's description of this process goes beyond the closing of our inner sight, foreshadowing its reopening:

> It is as if the psyche gradually crystallizes out of a nebular state in which it is distributed over the world. It then assumes form, becomes concentrated and centers down as the Self and the ego. Paradoxically, in the second half of life, though the process of crystallization is intensified, it is complemented, if we may continue the metaphor, by a kind of dissipation of the contoured form and a renewed extension of the range of the psyche till it again becomes co-terminous with the world and the unitary reality is restored."[3]

That is, the second half of life is described here as a progressive opening of the window onto eternity, provided there is sufficient earlier "crystallization."

Moreover, the person, whose ego has thus opened to the Self, and is no longer a "mere-ego" (an ego detached from its source), is now conscious of the entire process, and indeed sees a much fuller world.

NEUMANN EXPRESSES the visible world's formation as follows:

> The psyche apprehends both the so-called inner world and the so-called outer world *in terms of images* . . . Every . . . symbol, insofar as it has become an image, is already a creative psychic formulation, a mastering of the world by the creative psyche. The reality that lies behind these images is charged with an over-

[3] Neumann, *The Place of Creation.* p. 125.

> whelming, incomprehensible ... dynamism which impresses the psyche that is affected by it as a terrifying chaos and a menacing disorder. Every [apprehension of] reality in terms of images [enhances] security ... since it imposes order on the dynamic impact of anonymous outer and inner powers, and transforms them into a pattern accessible to us. This means not only that the unconscious [mirroring] process of image formation ... furthers the preservation of the species by assisting in our orientation in the world, but that the entire phenomenon of creativity in the psyche is governed by the constellation of order and form.[4]

That is, the very fact that we *see* is psychic creation. This is true of *fenestra aeternitatis* as well: we must have a psychic *reflector*, but now of a new sort. We must reflect; an activity that tends to increase with age and development. When we give our attention to the other side, we gradually find that we can see there, just as giving our attention to the visible world makes its sort of reality clearer to us also.

Opening to the Other Side

The fact that we *can* achieve a *vis à vis* with a portion of the total world-reality is an extension of the mystery of psychic reflection, or mirroring, but as Neumann points out, we have also run into certain limitations of the ego.

> As a result of the discovery by depth psychology of the relative dependence of the ego and the conscious mind on the complexes of the personal unconscious and the archetypes and instinctual structures of the collective unconscious, the classical psychology of freedom, based as it was on the conscious mind [was changed]. The emphasis was shifted to a more comprehensive psychic world, which includes the unconscious and the Self; the conception of a closed psychic system based on the conscious mind had to be surrendered in favor of one of a relatively open psychic world. This meant that when the creative connection, in sickness and in health, between the ego and the unconscious became the centerpoint of interest, the creative freedom of the psyche, and of the directing ego-Self axis within the psyche, was revealed as the basic principle of human existence.[5]

"To see the World in a grain of sand" is to have the window opened.[6] Dreams can be that opening as well, especially those that come with numinous feeling. When we resort to chance events for prophecy, even something as simple as flipping a coin, we intend to let the answer come from the other side. All games of chance (dice,

---

[4] Ibid., pp. 353–354.
[5] Ibid., pp. 352–353.
[6] William Blake. "Auguries of Innocence," from *Songs of Experience*. In *An Oxford Anthology of English Poetry*. 2d ed. New York: Oxford University Press, 1956. p. 537.

cards) are the same, letting the worldfield or the Self-field speak to our lives. Methods of divinization, such as use of the *I Ching,* Tarot, or astrology, are also methods of "reading the field." All forms of ESP also qualify as field effects, and manifest the field as mediator between person and person.

These experiences require something from us. We might say that the *world* becomes "transparent," but it may be equally true to say that it is *we* who become transparent. We say, for example, that the other side "shines through" certain persons whom we regard as saintly or charismatic. These individuals are those for whom the boundary between the two worlds, which usually seems so seamless and impenetrable to us, is less of a reality. In turn, they somehow mediate the other side to us; they are the transparent ones.

In 1787, William Blake tended his dying younger brother without sleep for two weeks, and after the death slept for three days and nights. He said that he saw the departing spirit of his brother clapping his hands for joy as he moved toward his new life. Later, he claimed that his brother showed him the key to the methods he later developed for combining his poetry and art in a single medium. When we say that we have seen a *spirit,* we usually refer to a contact with another living and intelligent being. Our example fits the meaning precisely: Blake said that he was in contact with the *spirit* of his brother.

This example, however, makes me question what happened to so many others in search of a solution to a problem (Kekule, Poincaré, Agassiz). In these cases, they immersed themselves in the details of the problem, and then something intervened to take their mind from it, intentionally or otherwise. Kekule and Agassiz received their solutions in dreams, visually. Kekule dreamed of a snake biting its own tail (the uroboros symbol), which was recognized as a metaphor for a carbon chain bending around and attaching ends to form a circle. This mythic dream none the less gave him the correct solution to a real problem in chemistry, the structure of benzene. The message to Agassiz was more direct. He simply dreamed the correct structure of a fossil fish, and found upon awaking that he had drawn it on the pad by his bed while asleep. Poincaré, while serving in the French army, one day stepped onto a bus with others, and immediately began seeing the mathematical equations over which he had been puzzling begin to rearrange themselves in a waking vision. He was able to remember all of this and to write the correct solution down later.

In the case of the scientists, we would probably say that the solution came from within themselves, but would we really say that it was different with Blake? In dreams, we speak to others, alive and dead, without the thought that we have had direct contact with the spirit of that person, for their image is a part of us. Why should it not be a mediating agent for that inner part of us that also works out the solution to the problem?

A few months before his mother died, C.G. Jung dreamed that his father came to him for marital counseling. After she died, Jung saw that the dream really was prophetic of her death, for it assumed that his father knew he would soon be living with her again. One could argue that all of this was "known" in Jung's unconscious, and that this was its means of coming to his consciousness. Jung took it, however, as an indication that the dead really do learn from us, and need us to help them acquire things in the evolution of knowledge. This might indeed occur whether or not we were aware of it happening. On the other hand, Swedenborg argued that a spirit in the other world has no more need of worldly knowledge, but only such knowledge as pertains to spiritual states, and that they are taught these things by other spirits more experienced in the things of the other side. This opens up considerations that are too broad for the present article. My own leaning, however, is toward the view that such visions represent what is currently happening in the psyche of the experiencing person, i.e., the one now living a physical life.

What we need in our lives is not to see how the other side was opened to so-called special people, such as the principal personages of the great religions, but to raise our own awareness of its presence in our own lives. Whether it is *actually* peopled by spirits of the departed, or whether that is only how we perceive the operation of the other side, is immaterial to the quality of our lives, though the *feeling* that spirits of the departed are helping us may be of tremendous importance to how we live. The other side helps us, whatever means it employs.

However, the "us" that it helps is rarely, if ever, the ego alone. In the current world, "empowerment" usually refers to ego-power. The field, however, is not something that can be manipulated to our egocentric ends. The ego-will must be overcome and assimilated by the greater reality of the Self.

This does not require "talent" but rather a creative *attitude.* Neumann recounts a Hasidic tale that explains why a "simple" man had a vision of Elijah, while a learned rabbi was denied such a vision:

> The simple man to whom Elijah had appeared had realized his small part of the soul of Elijah, whereas Ibn Ezra had not realized his much larger part.[7]

When we fulfill the meaning of our lives, we are no longer "mere-egos," or relative humans, but in some sense "absolute hu-

---

[7] Neumann, *The Place of Creation.* p. 374.

mans." In this sense, the Self would "appear" even to the single spore of slime mold that fulfilled its function. This is equivalent to saying that it is "absolute spore," and that the whole world-field is open to it, present to it. To adapt a statement that follows the tale in Neumann:

> The world-field is valid not only for humankind but for everything that lives and everything that exists, and that is the basis not only for all individual existence but of each thing that has been formed, in all its diversity, since it is everywhere one and the same reality. This means, however, that everything which fulfills its own nature is equal in rank and equal in radiance. [8]

What is required of us is not a turning away from the world, nor even turning toward the field, but looking at the invisible world through the veil of what we presently see as the visible world. As Neumann put it:

> Rembrandt was interested in making transparent the creative and formative quality that was the living, really effective background behind the foreground of the "objective" human reality and of the "objective" world. But this background of formless openness and formless form-creating activity shines through a landscape in a Chinese painting in the same way that it does through a Rembrandt.[9]

Our everyday world actually has a kind of transparency, through which the underlying reality of the whole invisible world becomes visible. We live within this reality at every moment, and we have the power to see that this is so.

Someone said, "In every direction, God *is*," to which we might add that in every direction God *can be seen*. Sometimes the sight of God is unbearable pain, as when we see meaning in human suffering, but also sometimes almost unbearable joy.

[8] Ibid., p. 375.
[9] Ibid., p. 379.

JOHN L. HITCHCOCK, a physicist who has been working in the field of science and spirituality for many years, is author of *Atoms, Snowflakes and God: The Convergence of Science and Religion*, and *The Web of the Universe: Jung, the New Physics, and Human Spirituality.* John has taught mythology as well as astronomy at San Francisco State University. Since 1968, he has led seminars with the Guild of Psychological Studies of San Francisco, specializing in mythology and in science as a source of numinous symbols. As an outgrowth of his interest in the worldfield, the nonrational background of physical reality, he has been a practicing astrologer for many years.

JAN FRAZIER

A Painting by Paul Gaugin, Seen in Winter

I want to dive into it, headfirst into
that clay-and-fern world. It is just there, so close,
just across the room and through that glass,

within that ample frame, ample enough
to lunge through. One step across the floor, one more
up and in, where everything is warm:

a clay road, women in their hats and scarves,
a thatched hut, an idling donkey, lush trees that rise
soft and green above and behind, and then,

largest and warmest of all, round, brown mountains,
mounds of comforting earth that push up
into the sky, push the blue out of the way

to make room for themselves. In a valley
far out there in the sun, I shall lie down,
press my face to the cool earth, and sleep

for years, waking because night has pulled day
behind the hills, sit up to find myself
in the gray of shade, and then shall hear

the sounds of the village—a guitar coming
from a porch, an old man calling to his wife—
and imagine (though I am too far out

to take it in) the scent of garlic and tomatoes
simmering in olive oil, bubbling rice
making the pot lid dance, and more, more,

bowls and spoons on the table, glasses of wine,
thick brown bread with a slab of butter, cheese.
Back out soon, though, for the stars are up,

and they always were there, but we forget,
in the glare of day we forget. We forget
it is possible to take one step

across a room, dive headlong into a painting,
curl up in a valley in the sun,
and wake to garlic and music and stars.

JAN FRAZIER, who lives in rural western Massachusetts, leads creative writing workshops in Vermont and Massachusetts. Her writing has been nominated for a Pushcart Prize. She has work in recent or forthcoming issues of *Negative Capability, Calyx, Minnesota Review, Artful Dodge, Poets On, Yankee, The Plum Review, High Plains Literary Review,* and *The Christian Science Monitor.* Her work has won awards and commendations in various poetry competitions.

Artist of the Apocalypse

Alexander Gassel

And in the spirit he carried me away to a great, high mountain, and showed me the holy city Jerusalem. . . . It had a great high wall, with twelve gates. . . . And the wall of the city had twelve foundations, and on them the twelve names of the twelve apostles of the Lamb.[1]

ST. JOHN'S VISION OF THE TRANSFORMED CITY springs from his own apocalyptic hope, but with cosmic breadth. In John's vision, Matth ew Fox finds the Cosmic Christ, a source of empowerment to Christi ans and non-Christians alike, and calls for a new mystical cosmology in which all humankind reaches the city.[2] For Swedenborg, twelve corresponds to all the holy things of faith, all things of truth and good. In the Episcopal Book of Common Prayer, New Jerusalem's twelve gates offer entry to all "sorts and conditions of men."

In our excitement over this salutary vision we easily overlook John's portrayal of the last things that precede the New Heavenly City, the evangelist's fearful apocalyptic events: ". . . I saw . . . a pale horse, and its rider's name was Death, and Hades followed him . . . behold, there was a great earthquake; and the sun became black as sackcloth, the full moon became like blood, and the stars of the sky fell to the earth. . . . [An angel] called out with a mighty voice, 'Fallen,

---

[1] *The New Oxford Annotated Bible with the Apocrypha.* New York: Oxford University Press, 1973. Revelation 21: 10a, 12a, 14.

[2] Matthew Fox. *The Coming of the Cosmic Christ.* San Francisco: Harper & Row, 1988. p. 99.

fallen is Babylon the great!'"[3] "Apocalypse" means "revelation"; John revealed his people's conditions in that day. He wrote from the prison island of Patmos, a prophet who "told it like it was" and yet offered hope of transformation.

Conditions in our own day arouse fear and despair. An easy refuge is materialism, in living for the moment, in enjoying what we can while we may. Our better selves rebel against such surrender. Sometimes our vision sees through our environment, beyond the material, to catch a message of metanoia. But our monkey minds leap away and frolic in novelties. Our time cries out for contemporary prophecy, a powerful revelation of our dire condition.

I found this revelation in the paintings of Alexander Gassel, born in Moscow in 1947. As some of my Russian friends have confirmed, children of that time were usually reared as atheist by atheist parents. A national ideal seized young hearts: equality, security, a paternal state. Gassel followed a path of idealism; his undergraduate double major was French and history of art. He told me that he had planned to work in Mali.

But fine art had rooted itself in his soul. His graduate study at Moscow's Institute of Art and Graphics was directed toward a doctorate in art history; then his career turned once more. I think he wanted to make his own art history, and he has done so. Abandoning the academic siren, he responded to his own developing talent and studied Fine Arts, training at the Grabar Restoration and Conservation Center, and the Stroganoff Art Graduate School. There Gassel mastered traditional methods of icon painting, which begins with a carefully prepared wooden panel. Fabric is glued to the board and covered with gesso. Following ancient practice, Gassel continued to grind his own pigments, which assures their fine crystalline structure. These are mixed with egg yolk, producing a rich color that must be applied quickly to achieve smooth layers of paint. Color areas are often enhanced by delicate hatching lines in contrasting color or gold.

Following graduation, Gassel worked from 1970 to 1980 at the prestigious Grabar Center restoring and preserving Russian icons that dated from the fifteenth through nineteenth centuries. His official career was icon restoration in churches and museums as directed by the Grabar Center. At the same time, he also developed a personal career, donating his restoration services to small rural churches. He tells me that these Christian communities impressed him with the quality of their clergy and concern for others' welfare. Touched by the spirit encountered in these small churches, Gassel began to

[3] *The New Oxford Annotated Bible*. Revelation 7:8a, 12, 13a, 18:2a.

Apocalypse. 25×41 inches. Private collection. The composition recalls the symmetry and imagery of old icons. Gassel has interpreted the Book of Revelation's symbols with dynamic energy and images: seven churches of Asia, seven spirits before the throne, dark clouds, seven golden lamp stands, someone seated on the throne in heaven, the four horse men, the slain Lamb nd the altar surrounded by twenty-four elders in white robes.

paint his own inspirations of Biblical subjects. His painting no longer stayed within the lines.

Apocalypse, painted in 1975 while he worked at icon restoration, brought a new dynamic quality to a traditional religious theme. The official hierarchy disapproved of Gassel's personal interpretations and labeled such art "illegal craftsmanship." For Russian artists, art is a community concern. Exhibits have always brought a cross-section of society; art is a part of social action.

With his life's work threatened, Gassel emigrated to the United States in 1980; he is now an American citizen. During the past fifteen years, he has continued to stretch the icon's technical boundaries.

Holocaust. 80×56 inches. Private collection. Gassel seduces us into this view of horrors with his dynamic composition and harmonies of crimson, violet, and gold. We cannot avoid closer examination. A slashing diagonal of brown-shirted troops directs the eye to the master of ceremonies: Death as Harlequin, spinning away lives on the central wheel of fortune. Above the wheel a band of marching troops gestures their power. Shades of Roman troops with gray helmets and ochre shields lean forward into a march beneath the imperious arm of a ghostly white Führer, a silhouette against a bloody panel that becomes a piercing triangle. Trampled by troops, a weary line of faded gray human beings struggles to their death under the eye of a guard in a tower. In contrast, the left side of the painting depicts what appears to be the failure of our religions. Two angels blow their vain trumpets from church towers, while their white and gold companions tumble into Death's abyss. An eternally crucified Christ falls toward disaster. Along the bottom a liturgical procession continues on its way: individuals bearing the head of Holophernes, Ark of the Covenant the Menorah and Torah, halting as bodies hurtle over a violet wall.

Gassel now uses the ancient technique of egg-yolk tempera for traditional and contemporary paintings. He makes his own color pigments by grinding natural stones and minerals into power that he then mixes with the egg yolk.

Gassel has moved from new versions of traditional subjects to new panoramas of spiritual morality plays, following his own vision of the Apocalypse. The Soviet Union's dissolution allowed acceptance of his art in the new Russia. In 1992 his work received a solo exhibition at the Central House of the Arts in Moscow.

A common friend introduced me to Gassel's work. His paintings from the 1980s spoke to my own aesthetic taste, which tends to be orderly and appreciative of churchly symbolism.

But in 1993 Gassel's style changed into apparently chaotic, wildly colorful dramas. My friend said, "These new paintings are difficult for me to understand." I agreed, but found myself gripped by the puzzles they presented. Pondering them, I began to see a development in Gassel's style that corresponds to Jung's distinction between psychological and visionary art. I also began to learn more about this artist of the Apocalypse.

The Last Battle. 68×48 inches. Marblehead, Massachusetts: St. Andrew's Episcopal Church. The wheel of fortune has become a black and gold circular raging battle. This time the troops are reduced; it appears that the battle is almost won. A line of chained white-robed figures mourns silently below soldiers with golden shields. The victors survey the carnage, accompanied by an approving Death riding a pale horse. Angels no longer sound trumpets but battle furiously as they are swept away in a whirlwind to fall into an abyss below a pile of wounded humanity. Little remains of religious institutions; church spires topple and a mother and child huddle together beside rape and pillage. A small group of souls to the left of the whirling battle makes futile gestures.

In Gassel's long series of apocalyptic works, I see artist as prophet: one who speaks forth to portray community concerns, who shows forth the state of a collective psyche of the community. His work in this series begins as consistent with Jung's notion of psychological art. For Jung, psychological art uses material from conscious life, with "crucial experiences, powerful emotions, suffering, passion, the stuff of human life in general." Psychological art raises the commonplace to the level of poetic experience, "giving us a greater depth of human insight by making us aware of those everyday happenings that we tend to evade or overlook."[4]

The Biblical Apocalypse, although dreadful, still contains the myth of the New Jerusalem and the saved. However, in Gassel's *Holocaust* (1989) no one is saved. Who would not like to deny the twentieth-century holocaust and its implications for human depravity? Gassel's holocaust is that of repeated history. On a lavender panel in the center of the painting, we find the preacher's weary warning, "What was will be again. What has been done will be done. There is nothing new under the sun."[5] The tragedy's glorious color is embellished with precious silver and gold. We would like to overlook life's enormous calamities, but we are drawn into this holocaust by its beauty of representation, only to be chilled by its images. Is this the dream of our collective psyche?

---

[4] C.G. Jung. *The Spirit in Man, Art, and Literature.* Princeton University Press, 1971. pp. 90–92.

[5] *The New Oxford Annotated Bible.* Ecclesiastes 1: 9.

Our fears are confirmed in *The Last Battle* (1990). As in the *Holocaust*, rose, white, and gold, embellished with crimson and pale violet, charm the eye and draw viewers willingly into the scene. Once engaged, we become fascinated as when we see the results of terrorism on the evening news or pass a bloody accident on the highway. This is powerful psychological art, engaging us with "crucial experiences, powerful emotions, suffering, passion, the stuff of human life in general," and in this case, a final culmination of human failure. In 1956 Jung wrote: "Everything now depends on man: immense power of destruction is given into his hand, and the question is whether he can resist the will to use it, and can temper his will with the spirit of love and wisdom."[6] Human hubris has made possible an ultimate holocaust.

Boston. 68×48 inches. Marblehead, Massachusetts: St. Andrew's Episcopal Church. The liturgical procession of Holocaust has become a line of lock-step consumers, clutching their purchases made from a shattered wagon. Emaciated horsemen ride forward into the familiar red Citgo sign, obscuring multiple Joe Camels. Icons of culture—Mona Lisa and Flora—serve business interests. Secular architecture commands center stage, surmounted by what may be a deformed gray Trojan horse. What gifts might it contain? Floating bits of fence fall to earth. A lone musician plays his saxophone beneath a bridge, alienated from a single figure behind him. Obscure religious remainders—American Gothic, a bit of Trinity Church, and a small Virgin in a blue shrine honored by three nuns—fade against material clamor of a cityscape. Near the nuns a juggler keeps things moving, and two women appear ready to practice the oldest profession.

Boston represents Gassel's contemporary themes painted in traditional tempera techniques, marked by the same subtle colors as *The Last Battle:* soft blue and green, rose and gold, sparked with black, white, and crimson. His view of the city is itself a revelation. Here is Boston, home of the Red Sox and the Apocalypse, familiar landmarks overridden with apocalyptic imagery.

---

[6] C.G. Jung. *Psychology and Religion: West and East.* Princeton University Press, 1958. p. 479.

This psychological art shows us the stuff of human life in general, but it seems that in capitalist cities few will recognize apocalyptic omens. Gassel's Boston is contained within a rectangular space and lacks the tornadoes of falling angels. Thus far the works have been framed. No longer.

Angel on the Bridge. 48×48 inches. Private collection. Where is the angel? Where is the bridge? A first impression shows a humanity reduced to grotesque heads and body fragments. Color is fully saturated; there are a few muted pinks and olive greens. There is no confining frame; these agonized forms cannot be contained. An infant form is intact but distorted. Once found, the angel has curled into powerlessness before the staring and threatening faces, and a broken green bridge leads to nothing. A few attenuated human figures in the center of the painting bow to a fragile pink and gold angelic chorus. Overpowering emotions of grief, sadness, anger, and despair register on human masks painted in vivid primary colors. Personality is reduced to an emotional essence. An occasional blue or gold hand reaches to nothing. One intact gray human face surveys the carnage from a blue area in the picture's center. This face looks very much like that of the creator of this chaotic tumbling array.

Since 1993 Gassel's icons have entered the realm of what Jung describes as visionary art: "everything is reversed, the material is no longer familiar."[7] The meaning of the work lies in "the visionary experience it serves to express."[8] Visionary art can be a revelation beyond understanding or beauty that we can never put into words. It is "as if it had emerged from the abyss of prehuman ages, or from a superhuman world of contrasting light and darkness . . . chilling the blood with its strangeness, it arises from timeless depths: glamorous, daemonic, grotesque, it bursts asunder our human standards of value and aesthetic form, a terrifying tangle of eternal chaos . . ."[9] We are reminded of dreams; "we demand commentaries and explanations."[10]

There is much repellent in *Angel on the Bridge* (1993): pain, disorder, distortion. But closer inspection reveals delicately decorated portions, a remnant from traditional icons. And because the tempera medium is in the hand of a master, the colors glow with their carefully prepared pigments. Despite an initial impression of chaos, we see that the viewer's eye is carefully led over

[7] Jung, *The Spirit in Man, Art, and Literature.* p. 90.
[8] Ibid., p. 92.
[9] Ibid., p. 90.
[10] Ibid., p. 91.

Lost City. 46×48 inches. Private collection. Our own golden patriotic icon, the Father of our Country, stands above the city's destruction. But he is aloof to the situation. He gazes into space and pets his horse. Other three-dimensional gold figures curl into available space. No homes remain—only façades of gold, gray, and blue. Bits of railings float over the surface. What appear to be three cast-off tires stabilize the bottom corner. These tires will not travel. An isolated figure plays his music. Lives do not connect. At the bottom of the ruin we see what appears as a tragic domestic event. A blue figure of a man leans with a whip over the fallen body of a woman in a red dress; nearby stands a broken chair. A door of a gentle pink building hangs loose and reveals a lone light bulb. It is dark. We see beyond the chaos of this lost city open air, clouds, light, and a rosy sailing kite. This is a view that restores hope, until we see that the only vegetation is a dead gray tree and there is no one to sail the kite. The kite is lost. The city suffers its death throes. The city is lost.

the surface, guided by brilliant red areas, sweeps of green, spots of gold, accented with pure black and white. The meaning of the work lies in "the visionary experience it serves to express," a nonverbal meaning to which we make our own emotional responses as to another apocalyptic drama.

Lost City (1994) seems to return us to Boston, now a rubble of disintegration. This apocalypse is close to home. A new element appears in golden three-dimensional figures that provide only occasional containment of a tumbling, fragmented human world. The last battle has been fought, the legions of warriors reduced to domestic violence. All order is lost. Abandon hope. Gassel's latest visionary works charm us with color and design, but reveal a world broken beyond our understanding. We have been thrown into an prehuman abyss, into timeless depths, into a terrifying tangle of eternal chaos. Gassel has said that he paints despair; we no longer struggle to uphold our ideals. We have abandoned hope. But Alexander Gassel is also a prophet of hope.

Jung has described the mission and work of a visionary artist. Like prophets and seers, Gassel is in touch with the night side of life and nourished by it. The artist "now and then catches sight of the figures that people the night-world—spirits, demons, and gods; he feels the secret quickening of human fate by a suprahuman design, and has a presentiment of incomprehensible happenings in the pleroma (the divine fullness)."[11] The visionary artist foretells "changes in the conscious outlook of his time."[12] He has "plunged into the healing and redeeming depths of the collective psyche . . . where all men are caught in a common rhythm which allows the individual to communicate his feelings and strivings to mankind as a whole."[13]

Gassel shows us the ephemeral nature of our false material gods. Although we have built a manageable daytime world of consciousness, unconscious terrors clamor in the night. We are warned against spiritual destruction. To become whole people, we must integrate our unconscious contents, not deny them.

As Jung says, "The work of the artist meets the psychic needs of the society in which he lives, and therefore means more than his personal fate, whether he is aware of it or not. . . . He has done his utmost by giving it form and must leave the interpretation to others and to the future. A great work of art is like a dream." Like a dream, "it presents an image . . . and it is up to us to draw conclusions."[14]

Gassel forces on our vision the seductive beauty of his apocalyptic drama. He opens the gates of our unconscious, the chaotic birthing place of our creative energy, of change and hope. The eternal New Jerusalem awaits us, not only in the future, but in each present eternal moment. Guided by contemporary prophets, we can confront our apocalyptic fears and discover the twelve gates of an ecumenical paradise wherein we welcome the image of God into our souls.

[11] Ibid., p. 96.
[12] Ibid., p. 99.
[13] Ibid., p. 105.
[14] Ibid., p. 104.

KATHERINE STANNARD lives in Massachusetts, travels to Moscow and St. Petersburg, and has found new friends through the Worcester–Pushkin Sister City Project. She is professor emerita of psychology at Framingham State College. Paintings by Alexander Gassell are found in Vatican City, the Ryazan and Kirillov Art Museums in Russia, the Episcopal Divinity School in Cambridge, Massachusetts, and in St. Leo's parish in Stamford, Connecticut. Over a hundred paintings and drawings are in private collections in the United States, Germany, France, Holland, Russia, Israel, and Syria.

WILLIAM C. HONEY

Tiene Fósforo?

IT WAS THE LAST NIGHT of my friends' visit to Puerto Rico. We sat on the patio of the Lutece guest house sipping pina coladas and listening to the sound of the waves breaking on the sandy beach on the other side of the patio wall. I was sorry to see my friends leave. Their visit had been a pleasant interlude in my life in a small apartment in the west end of the island of Puerto Rico where I taught English at the Colegio de Mayagüez.

The man was a painter and sculptor, and his wife was an artist in managing a large household on an income that fluctuated wildly with the fashions of art sales. I had taught them to snorkle over a shallow reef and to enjoy the pleasures of hot bread from the panaderia after a day in the water. We sipped our drinks and listened to the waves.

"Why is the north side of the island so different from the other side, where you live?" the man asked.

"Because this side of the island faces on the Atlantic Ocean and the other side faces the Caribbean Sea," I answered. "The Atlantic is colder and deeper." We sat in silence for a moment and contemplated the depths of the oceans and the late winter light that was fading.

It was a typical winter evening, almost cool enough for a light sweater, and clear because the rainy season was several months away. In a few minutes the sun would suddenly disappear into the water with a burst of afterlight.

As soon as the afternoon light faded, the tourists who stayed in the big hotels along the beach retreated inside to wash off their suntan lotion and prepare for an evening in the casinos. They were missing the best part of the day.

Nights in Puerto Rico are beautiful. The air is soft and inviting, with just enough coolness to compensate for the warmth of the sun during the day. The stars seem innumerable, even near the hotel area where the marquee lights are bright.

The woman suddenly put her drink down and announced, "I want to walk on the beach."

"It's too late for that," I said. "The beach is deserted. Everyone has gone inside. Order another drink instead."

"I like the beach better this way," she said, standing and slipping off her sandals. "Without the tourists."

"I'll go with you," the man said, and stood also. "We can have the beach to ourselves. It will be more romantic."

"Come on Bill. Don't be a party pooper," she said to me.

I wanted to talk them out of this idea. I was happy on the patio. The conversation was pleasant, and I didn't like idea of walking on the beach at night.

"We don't usually walk on the beach at night," I started to say. "There are problems . . ." But they had already started for the opening in the patio wall that led to the beach.

At this hour the beach would be deserted, and the hotel security people would be inside watching the gamblers. The lights of the big hotels did not extend out to the beach, but were directed to the loungers at the tropical bar on the deck around the swimming pool.

"Come on Bill," I heard my friends shout from the beach. They were not going to come back, so I slipped out of my chair and joined them.

Lutece was a small guest house situated between the large hotels of the Condado and Isle Verde, a residential area where Pablo Casals lived. My friends had turned west to walk along the beach adjacent to the big hotels.

All the tourist hotels had built raised swimming pools on the beach side with tall sea walls. Flood lights on the sides of each hotel illuminated the pool area, but created deep shadows in the lee of the sea wall and did not penetrate beyond the sea wall to the beach.

As we walked along the water's edge the sand and the water were cool on the bottoms of our bare feet. The tide was receding, and the usual interesting shells and other flotsam of the ocean that had been washed up during high tide were now exposed. My friends were having a great time. I was still nervous and kept an eye on the shadows beneath the sea walls as we walked further and further away from the safety of the Lutece.

We reached a point where the beach curved outward into the Atlantic. Because of the radical curve of the beach, anyone approaching us had a favorable angle whether we walked forward or back toward Lutece. I felt someone was now walking parallel to us in the shadow of the sea wall.

My friends stopped to investigate an object on the beach. While my friends argued what the object was, a man emerged from the dark shadow of the sea wall and began to walk directly toward us. I couldn't tell who he was or how large he was because the lights from the hotel shined on his back and put the front of his body entirely in shadow.

I watched the figure walking toward us reach into his pants pocket with his right hand and pull out an object that he flicked outward with his wrist. Open, the object glittered when the lights from the hotel caught the edge of the blade.

"Excuse me," I said to my friends. "I have to talk to this man. I'll be right back."

My friends looked at me quizzically and then returned to their observations of things washed up on the beach. I was afraid the night and the strange language might cause my friends to panic, which might cause the man with the knife to panic, and then I knew that bad things could happen that nobody really wanted. I decided to meet the man in a neutral space where he would be free not to hurt anyone.

I turned and walked straight across the sand toward the man.

We met halfway between the water's edge and the sea wall, and stopped when we were less than half a meter apart. I maneuvered to where he could see my face clearly in the hotel lights, and I could see his face partially. He was in control, and I thought it was important that he see that I was calm and not threatening.

This closeness of people standing for ordinary conversation is part of the Puerto Rican culture, and I was used to it after three years of living on the island. Neither of us felt invasive of the other's space even though by United States standards we stood close enough to be "in one another's face."

The man was Puerto Rican, in his middle twenties, with light skin and a thin frame. Like me, he was about five foot nine. I was heavier and in better condition, but he had the knife. He wore cheap, dark pants, a flowered tourist shirt open three buttons down the chest, and shoes without socks or laces. I guessed he lived in one of the barrios close to the Condado because the San Juan police patrol the streets entering the tourist area carefully.

I carefully reached into my shirt pocket with my right hand and pulled out a package of Marlboros. He watched quietly with the hand that held the knife hung loosely at his right side where the knife blade was partly hidden by his trousers.

I flicked a cigarette up from the pack and put the pack to my mouth and extracted the cigarette with my lips. Then I flicked out another, still holding the package with my right hand, and held the pack toward him. He reached out and took a cigarette with his left hand and put it in his mouth.

"Tiene fósforo?" I asked. Do you have a match?

I waited while he thought about my request. It was a long time before he answered. I was obviously a gringo, but it was a reasonable thing to ask, and it was said in Spanish.

Finally he put his left hand into his pants pocket and brought out a book of paper matches. It takes two hands to light a paper match on a windy beach. In his right hand he still held the knife. I waited patiently for him to decide what he was going to do. Finally he put his right hand behind his leg, where he pushed the button that loosens the blade, and closed the blade by pushing the back side of the sharp edge against his leg so the blade slid into the handle of the knife. Then he put his hand into his pant's pocket and brought the hand out again without the knife.

He took the book of paper matches in both hands and scraped the paper match on the cover until it lit. He cupped both his hands around the flame to protect it against the wind off the ocean. He held out his cupped hands, and I leaned forward so the flame touched the end of the cigarette that I held in my mouth.

When we were both lit, we each took a deep puff and exhaled. I raised my head and blew smoke into the night sky. For a long time we each inhaled and exhaled and examined the end of our cigarettes for ashes.

Finally I broke the silence and asked him, "Tiene dinero?" Do you have any money?

He shrugged his shoulders and put both palms outward. "No," he replied.

I reached into my back pocket and pulled out my wallet. Tilting the wallet toward him and the light from the hotel so he could see inside the bill compartment I extracted two ten dollar bills. He could see the compartment was empty.

"Tengo viente dollores. No mas." I said that I had twenty dollars, and no more.

He shook his head affirmatively. He could see that it was true.

"Equalmente," I said and held one of the ten dollar bills toward him.

He took the bill. "Gracias," he said in a low voice, but he was slow in putting the bill into his pocket, and he watched me carefully. Perhaps he thought there is no accounting for the behavior of gringos, but the money is good to have without forcing it.

"No soy touristo. Soy Puerto Ricano." I said I was not a tourist but a Puerto Rican, enunciating my Spanish as well as I could.

He looked at me without belief.

"Puerto Ricano," I added. "En my corazón." I pointed to my heart to show him my feeling for the island known as Borinquen was strong.

This he understood. "Sí," he acknowledged with a shrug.

Our business seemed to be done, and he started to shuffle his feet in the sand. He was anxious to return to the darkness along the sea wall. This was an area for tourists, and he did not want the *policia* to find him there. It might be rough for him to be found in this area.

I felt good. The meeting had gone well. The knife was put away. No incident had spoiled the visit of my friends. I was ten dollars poorer, but that was just money.

Then the instinct that had successfully guided me into this encounter began to desert me.

"Señor!" I said sharply.

He turned quickly to face me. Had the gringo changed his mind? Did he want his money back? Were the *policia* coming? He was suddenly defensive and the ease that had existed between us was gone. He waited cautiously for me to speak.

I was taken back by the change in him, and I had nearly exhausted my command of Spanish. I wanted to ask him about himself, but I didn't know how to ask. Perhaps I wanted more of this man than he was willing to give and my knowledge of Spanish would allow. So I held out the package of cigarettes toward him and asked, "Quiere mas cigarios?" Do you want more cigarettes?

The sharpness left my voice, and he returned to where I stood and took the pack from my outstretched hand without acknowledging the question.

"Amigo?" I said softly.

"Amigo," he replied even more softly, and turned and walked quickly away into the shadow of the sea wall and was gone.

It was not true that we were *amigos*. We had met briefly on a dark beach and shared a cigarette. That was all.

WILLIAM C. HONEY is professor of Legal Studies at Auburn University at Montgomery. He enjoys writing, reading, and sailing.

STEPHEN AND ROBIN LARSEN

Masks of the Spirit

Symbolic Consciousness from Swedenborg to Campbell

THE THOUGHT of Emanuel Swedenborg anticipated the work of Carl Jung and Joseph Campbell, particularly in the understanding of symbolic consciousness and an emerging attitude toward the spiritual life in today's global culture. Between the late eighteenth century, when Swedenborg's work began to be known, and the end of the twentieth, lies an incredible period of intellectual and technical growth that paved the way to the "postmodern" world. The influence of Swedenborg's thought has been less apparent in the formal disciplines of theology or philosophy but rather appeared in a thousand different ways spanning the arts, literature, psychology, and social philosophy, that during those two-hundred years transformed European and American culture in ways far more profound than those of many better known contributors.

Our thesis here is that both the work and the life of Emanuel Swedenborg contain key symbolic or paradigmatic elements in a major shift in the spiritual climate of Western civilization. This change is indispensable to our continued evolution and growth, and represents an antidote to some of the most destructive elements in Western religion. Perhaps we could introduce the problem with a couple of criticisms—in the form of stories—from another culture zone: the East.

The first is an apocryphal story told of Mahatma Gandhi, the great pacifist and social reformer who brought the Indian nation out of colonialism into independence. Someone asked Gandhi what he thought of Western civilization. He replied, "I think it would be a good idea!" For all of its vaunted technological achievements, Western civilization has seemed, from the viewpoint of Eastern wisdom, terribly callow in the zone of psychospiritual development, and because of this immaturity, barbarous in its wielding of social and political *force majeur.*

The second story was one of Joseph Campbell's favorites. He was attending one of the multicultural Eranos Conferences in Switzerland when Daisetz T. Suzuki, an important interpreter of Japanese culture to the West was asked for his opinion of Western religion. In a characteristic gesture, the diminutive philosopher rubbed his hands on his hips and wrinkled his brow. "Let's see. God against Man, Man against God. God against Nature, Nature against God, Man against Nature, Nature against Man; very funny religion!"

Seen from the outside, and from the perspective of Suzuki's sophisticated Taoist, Shinto, and Buddhist sources, Western religion, failing to understand the dynamism of opposing forces in nature, and the possibility of a profound symbiosis between the natural, the human, and the divine, had assumed a pathological, dualistic stance. Starting from the elemental dualism of good and evil, the polarities persisted and extended to the human relationship to the divine, and the divine as present in the world. Still more important from a psychological point of view has been the human relation to nature, and especially our own nature, "human nature." The outcome of these dualistic dichotomies is visible everywhere in Western civilization—in our existential guilt and depression before the image of a wrathful, legalistic God; in our myths of a nature that must be conquered and subdued rather than worshiped, learned from, and respected; and in our own sad alienation from our own biological and instinctive life, so well described in Freud's *Civilization and its Discontents.*

Now, Suzuki was talking about the historically dominant thrust of Judeo–Christianity, for which Swedenborg's far more interactive model offers a rectifying compensation, as we shall see. Suzuki did, in fact, read Swedenborg closely, and paid him a high compliment, calling him "The Buddha of the North."

But first we must look at the ways in which religions influence cultures. It is this theme that is implicit in our title: Masks of the Spirit. During the 1950s and 60s Joseph Campbell wrote a monumental tetralogy of religious experience, which he titled *The Masks of God.* What are the "masks" of his treatment? They are the myths themselves, said Campbell. As human beings we have no way of beholding the divine directly. All we see or know are our own (symbolic) representations. These "masks," or metaphors, enable us to personify, and thus to begin to imagine or conceptualize some aspects of what is essentially beyond us, the "Mysterium Tremendum et Fascinans" so termed by historian of religion, Rudolph Otto. The danger is the almost universal tendency to literalization. We mistake the mask for that which it implies, and then our image does just the reverse, occluding our ability to see spiritually.

"And why should it be," asks Campbell in his prologue, "that whenever men have looked for something solid on which to found their lives, they have chosen not the facts with which the world abounds, but the myths of an immemorial imagination, preferring

Count Erik Dahlberg. *Riddarhuset.* Engraving, 1716. As eldest male in his generation of the family, Swedenborg was entitled to a seat in the Riddarhuset (House of Nobles), which he attended diligently for fifty-three years.

even to make life a hell for themselves and their neighbors, in the name of some violent god, to accepting gracefully the bounty that the world affords?"[1]

Campbell was referring to the fact that about three-quarters of the bloody conflicts on the planet are 'religious wars,' waged by people who prefer the literal form of one mask of the spirit to another.

This idea is fundamental to understanding the spiritual crisis of our time. "It has been customary with some to exhibit representations, especially of holy things," writes Swedenborg in his *Spiritual Diary,* "and to institute certain spectacular displays of sacred things. Exhibitions of this sort are not allowable because the idea of them remains after death, and by those who are profane this is turned into profane representations," he says.[2] We know of no better statement

[1] Joseph Campbell. *The Masks of God.* Vol.1, *Primitive Mythology.* New York: Viking Press, 1959. p. 4.

[2] Emanuel Swedenborg. *The Spiritual Diary,* paragraph no. 233.

in Swedenborg's writings on the danger of symbolic literalism. It is merely a psychological version of the making of "graven images," which Judaism, an essentially aniconic (imageless) religion, evidently found so distasteful in the other Mesopotamian religions. The mask of God is a device to help us visualize, to turn our earthly vision into a spiritual kind of seeing, but not to be revered as the thing itself to be worshiped. This is idolatry.

In a scholarly paper, "The Symbol without Meaning," presented at an Eranos Conference, Joseph Campbell writes,

> We cannot forget the distinction between sign and symbol defined by Dr. Jung: the sign is a reference to something known; the symbol is a figure by which allusion is made to an unknown. It is, then, into the unknown, beyond both the image of god and the image of man, that we must venture to find the ultimate ground of all these guiding and protecting, edifying yet imprisoning, names and forms.[3]

In his most trenchant criticism of Swedenborg's "doctrine of correspondences", R.W. Emerson said essentially the same thing: "The slippery is not so easily caught. In nature each individual symbol plays innumerable parts.... Nature is no literalist.... She avenges herself on hard pedantry that would chain her waves."[4] For Swedenborg everything in nature, or in the natural world that appears in Scripture, had a specific theological and doctrinal meaning. It seems that for Emerson this aspect of Swedenborg's thought succumbed to the same thing he was trying to cure, symbolic literalism. But Emerson's criticism may also have been meant more for the orthodox Swedenborgians than for Swedenborg.

Recently a paradigm has emerged that may help us explain the extraordinary potency that images have on cultures and culture epochs. Rupert Sheldrake, the visionary biologist, whose work has very recently become quite influential, called it "morphic" or "morphogenetic resonance." Stated quite simply, perhaps the remarkable gains of biological evolution are not just the effects of Darwinian *natural selection,* but could be accomplished by a transfer of information that passes directly from mind to mind, through image and symbol. When a few, or a critical number of individuals of a species learn a new behavior, the effect transfers to the entire species.

Sheldrake has observed the phenomenon in such annoying, but amusing commonplaces as the ways in which starlings remove the paper tops of milk bottles, sitting on a hundred-thousand doorsteps

---

[3] Joseph Campbell. *The Flight of the Wild Gander.* New York: The Viking Press, 1969. p. 157.

[4] Quoted in Eugene Taylor. "Emerson: The Swedenborgian and Transcendentalist Connection." In *Emanuel Swedenborg: A Continuing Vision.* New York: Swedenborg Foundation, 1988. p. 133.

in the British Isles. At first the technique, never seen heretofore, that allowed the birds to remove the top and drink the milk at the neck of the bottle, was quite restricted; but soon, within a matter of a few weeks, much to everyone's dismay, the phenomenon had spread throughout the Isles, even to Wales, Scotland, and Ireland, and in a way far more rapidly than could be explained by mere imitation. Yes, the birds are smarter than we gave them credit for, but here their collective genius seemed diabolically threatening to British milk drinkers.

But, even if we make the assumption that the principle of morphic resonance does exist among animal species, you might say, isn't it either bold or demeaning to imagine that it might exist among human beings? Aren't we a breed apart from animals? Perhaps, but aren't there also universal ideas, themes, symbols, habits, to which the human mind is susceptible, and that sweep through communities, cultures, and epochs? To this proposal, the thought of Swiss psychologist Carl Jung offers a resounding, "Yes!"

Contemporary opinion sees collective manifestations usually as being culturally or socially propagated. But if one pays close attention to the ways in which such images work, we human beings seem to be haunted by mythic themes that emerge from something very much like Jung's "Collective Unconscious." I (Stephen) remember in the nineteen sixties wishing I could find some bell-bottomed trousers—but there were none in the stores. I also liked those little wire-rimmed spectacles that were thought to be archaic or old-fashioned. Then suddenly, they erupted into the collective mindscape—along with a whole host of related ideas—the peace movement, tribalism, living in tepees, driving an old hearse with rainbow decals, and other quaint fantasies. I saw with astonishment images and ideas that I had privately nursed now walking and dancing through the external landscape. Nowadays it's having lavender hair that comes to a point, or an orange "Mohican," or rings in one's nose or lips as well as ears that seems to appeal to many. Each era, even each decade, seems to have its own symbols that speak to something in the collective mind of the time.

To adduce morphic resonance as the sole factor in such movements of imagery in the modern world would seem unnecessary, because of the pervasive role of communication media. But let us imagine for the sake of argument that human beings are even more susceptible to morphically transmitted image and idea than our animal brethren. In part this is due to our larger brains and our culture-disseminated symbolic systems, which include not only language and customs, but also art forms, musical styles, and those elaborate narrative symbologies we call "myths." Both Joseph Campbell and psychologist Jerome Bruner have pointed out that until we have been able to make a story or a narrative out of our own experience, we cannot really process it very well psychologically, (so we say "I arrived on the scene with no expectations but then he said this, and I couldn't let it pass, so I did that . . .") Bruner calls this "the narratizing function" of consciousness. Culture and life are thus held together by a tissue of meaning-imbued images and narratives. Beethoven became deaf, but his magnificent symphony music came from all the previous experiences that embodied the spirit of his understanding up to that point in his life. He sensed the spirit of the music and was able to communicate it even though he was deaf and couldn't hear it on a physical level. It was within him. When we create something, it is a representation of our story. If it has integrity, it communicates to others. For Beethoven, it was a symphony. For a Native American, it could be an actual mask of a spirit or ancestor or a narrative or ceremony that expresses his relation to the spirit.

Psychologist Jean Houston has said that mythologies are the RNA of human culture, formative systems that shape our values and our experience of life. In another analogy, drawn from computers, if the brain and the nervous system are the hardware, myths and symbols are the software of human experience, without which we have no way of finding the meaning inherent in living. But these meanings, like RNA and DNA, operate at subconscious levels of influence. We are often moved by images and narratives without knowing why. Is it possible, then, that we don't think and feel things merely because the culture presents them to us, as the materialistic paradigm suggests, but that the myths and values that inform cultures, like dreams, arise from the depths, and because they are collective, appeal to many human minds at the same time? In effect, we dream our culture and our world onward.

Recently I (Stephen) was speaking with a Zulu *Sangoma* (shaman), Credo Mutwa, with whom I have just finished writing a book called the *Song of the Stars.* (Credo is reachable by telephone in Africa through what Robin and I jokingly call our "dial-a-witchdoctor-service.") He was commenting on those acts of terrorism which seem to shake the very foundations of our world—particularly the Oklahoma bombing and the nerve-gassing in the Japan subways.

"There is a deep apocalyptic delusion spreading throughout humanity, Doctor Stephen," he said in his characteristic way. I began to attend very closely. "Tell all of your friends and loved ones, and those with whom you come in contact, to pray for humanity right now. The delusion arises from deep within the brain in those parts that are not conscious, and it fills some people with a terrible desire that they can only come to the next stage of evolution by doing violence."

They may think they want to do good, but the only way they can see to get there is through this evil of violence against what now exists."

As he spoke I thought of Yeats' apocalyptic lines: "The best lack all conviction, while the worst / Are full of passionate intensity."[5]

For this Zulu wise man, there was no difficulty at all in believing that vast dreams of apocalypse and transformation sweep through the brains of humanity, affecting them in different but analogous ways. Some see violence as the only way to be reborn, others envision a more gentle transformation. Some think we can only move happily into the new millennium if we have a clean and wholesome environment, others only if we free industry from galling restrictions, so that the economy can flourish. Some think we can improve humanity only by returning to the fundamentals of religious tradition, others by revolutionizing and breathing new life into the religious experience. But let us now reflect on these dynamics during the eighteenth century.

At the inception of that vast cognitive revolution called the European Enlightenment, one of the pivotal questions was, "*Where do we look for the most authoritative revelation of what is real?*"—Do we look to Holy Writ, as had seemed unquestionable until that time, or into the world of phenomena itself, approached in that radically new way we now term the scientific method? Just before Swedenborg's time, things had progressed to a kind of impasse. We all know of the enormous influence upon European culture of Descartes, who lived his last years in Sweden and died there. In Sweden, after Descartes, science was newly empowered to be used and taught in all areas of inquiry, except religion and those things belonging to theology. The morphic field of Europe was changing, and theology no longer was the Queen of Sciences who could dictate truth to all others—her demesne was now to be restricted to the interpretation of scriptures and the celebration of holy sacraments.

Swedenborg's father, Jesper, Bishop of Skara, was in many respects a worldly and urbane man, but when it came to the central authority of the Scriptures, there was for him no doubt as to the potency and integrity of the literal Biblical message. But his young son, Emanuel, felt no urge to follow his charismatic father into the pulpit. Instead, Emanuel turned his remarkable intelligence to furthering the revelations of this new way of knowing called "science." He studied what would now be identified as chemistry, mineralogy, biology, archaeology, physics, astronomy, and mathematics (the boundaries between those disciplines being not nearly so well established as in contemporary times).

---

[5] William Butler Yeats. "The Second Coming." In *The Poems of W.B. Yeats.* Edited by Richard J. Finneran. New York: Macmillan Publishing Co., 1983. p. 187.

Swedenborg then passed through a spiritual crisis in his mid-fifties and began to turn his attention wholly to the spiritual life and a new interpretation of Scripture. The seminal, world-transforming ideas that he presented to the culture of his time have permeated Western thinking ever since. Were they in fact a revelation from the divine itself, the spiritual sense of the holy "Word," accompanying the second coming of Christ in the spiritual world, through the servant of the lord, Emanuel Swedenborg, as he averred?

Octagon Room, Royal Observatory in Greenwich. Eighteenth-century engraving. Just after graduation from Upsala University in 1709, Swedenborg made his first of many trips abroad. He was looking for advanced engineering study opportunities. One turned up at the Royal Observatory in Greenwich, where Swedenborg became assistant to the Master Astronomer.

The opposing view is expressed in Kant's patronizing *Dreams of a Spirit Seer;* the idea that Swedenborg's demonstrably brilliant intellect, encountering a mid-life crisis, suddenly reverted, perhaps through a psychological regression, to his father's original life plan. Thereafter Swedenborg's introverted tendency deepened, and he traveled through the spiritual worlds, heaven and hell, and spent the rest of his life writing repetitively about his visions, but relating everything back to the authority of the scriptures!

Another view of Swedenborg's transformation returns us to our thesis, and even offers to accommodate the data in a way that the New Physics has called "paradoxical." Werner Heisenberg's Uncertainty Principle tells us that all perspectives in science cannot help but include the viewpoint of the perceiver. If one is biased toward measuring particles, light appears to be made up of "photons." If one thinks of light as waves, it is easy to find filters and refraction indices that clearly justify light's wavelike oscillations. (In Jungian terms, the myth unconsciously held by the perceiver bends the data under observation into a subtly biased interpretation congruent with the unconscious myth.) If one thinks theologically, Swedenborg's revelation is unquestionably divine in origin; otherwise how could it contain those luminous truths that have touched many generations, and reach our minds and hearts even today? If one thinks psychologically, how could it be otherwise than that Swedenborg's religiously imbued childhood influenced his mid-life *recursion,* and even that aspects of his father's theology are discernible in certain of his revealed spiritual "doctrines?" It has also been noted that Swedenborg's pre-theological and post-theological ideas are not so easily separable (i.e., there are many anticipations of the latter in the former).

Our thesis is similar to the paradoxical viewpoint that modern physics has found inescapable. Is it possible that not only Swedenborg's crisis and "enlightenment," but his very biography itself was precipitated out of the morphic field of his time? Is it possible that Swedenborg's personal psychological journey into chaos and regeneration, death and rebirth, his biography itself, anticipates holographically the seeds of a new spiritual revelation, religious roots for a new church for the new millennium?

What is indisputable is how Swedenborg's personal mythology includes, in microcosmic form, questions that were pivotal for his time (as well as our own): the origin of the solar system—or the universe—the nature of matter, the search for the seat of the soul, the spiritual meanings contained within the Bible apart from its role as an historical document of a "chosen people," the idea of a developmental psychology for the mature human psyche (regeneration), the proper human relationship to nature, inner and outer, and many others. We are going to argue nothing less than that Swedenborg, in his life and in his work, embodied an embryonic mythology of the new millennium, and by living it through, changed our morphogenetic field, thus anticipating the morphology of the next psychospiritual transformation for humankind.[6]

SWEDENBORG'S LIFE AND WORK endeavored to introduce a compensation to some of the more distorted masks of the spirit prevalent in the European theology of his time. According to the model we are proposing, certain forms held to in the morphic field, forms influencing the human idea of the divine, literally became pathologies, with serious spiritual and psychological consequences—in individual lives and in the culture. What were some of these?

[6] Sheldrake also calls such a morphogenetic field a field of "formative causation."

Perhaps foremost was the Trinitarian concept that a righteous God sent down his son down as a sacrifice for the sins of humanity. Swedenborg addresses this concept perhaps more than any other theological issue in his writing. The (symbolically) theological cure he proposes? Simply that Jesus, the "son," was an aspect, not a separate person, of the merciful Godhead, who intended the Christian Incarnation as a great moral lesson in what it means to be fully human, not an inhuman sacrifice. Swedenborg felt that this one shift of emphasis would make an enormous change in the Christian religion.

A second idea concerned heaven and hell as places of reward and punishment (a punitive model based on divine wrath and judgment). Heaven and hell do exist, Swedenborg acknowledged in perhaps his most famous book, *Heaven and Hell;* but they are not places of reward and punishment, rather they are conditions of the soul present even in the here and now, as an individual follows his or her primary motivational system or "ruling love." When the outermost sheath, the physical body is shed, the soul gravitates to a spiritual zone with which it is most consistent, and most comfortable. To the inhabitants of both heaven and hell, the other zone seems like "hell"—a place vastly inimical to one's own inner state. The divine does not punish, but allows limitless choices to all souls. Swedenborg felt that this doctrine alone could introduce a psychological dimension to the experience of religion and reduce the painful ideation of guilt and retribution that seems to haunt Christianity. (Had this concept really taken hold in the eighteenth century, it probably could have rendered the practice of Christianity comparable, by now, to the most sophisticated Eastern spiritual practices.) It is an idea that is very present in Creation Spirituality and others of the most radical contemporary interpretations of Christianity.

A third idea pertained to what constitutes the life of religion. Swedenborg probably saw even more public piety and religious ostentation than we do today. But true spirituality has nothing to do with these kinds of observances, he said, challenging the world's sense of ecclesiastical propriety. Instead, "the life of religion is to do good." Attuning ourselves to the needs of others, we pass along in a practical way the inexhaustible spiritual bounty which is vouchsafed us as living children of God. Taking this idea to its furthermost expression, the human community creates Heaven on Earth through charitable action. This is certainly the foundation of philanthropic Humanism, and it returns the locus of spirituality from a divine that lies beyond comprehension to the human community.

According to Swedenborg, external behavior is meaningless without reference to spiritual intention, or inward orientation to the divine source. The "mask" of the spirit, if it conceals one's true motives, is just that: a mask, a disguise. Here is a way to understand hypocrisy: What you do matters less, on a spiritual level, than what you intend to do. Behind this is Swedenborg's profound idea of the Divine Influx that sustains all living things. In and of ourselves we are merely "receptacles," hollow vessels for the spiritual energy that streams ceaselessly from the Divine Core of the Universe, sustaining every living thing. This fourth doctrine is an idea not only consistent with the subtlest insights of Taoism and Buddhism, but with all of Oriental Medicine, where health is equivalent to opening ourselves to universal energy *(chi)* that sustains our vitality. Swedenborg begins one discussion with the following heading: "A spiritual paradox: that in man, especially in his internals, there is nothing but a fluid stream like the breath *(Spiritus)* . . ."[7] This is exactly the life energy (*chi, prana, pneuma*) that is believed to flow with the breath and sustain the vital organs and the entire subtle energy field of the body. Swedenborg's words could be taken from a text of *Qi Gong*, the ancient Chinese art of healing by energy. He says that anything hard is brittle, external, "and would quickly perish," and that as we move toward the internals, the "spiritual substances" are more and more fluid and subtle; only the most exterior gives the semblance of solidity. This insight also offers a theoretical structure for psychosomatics. The mind and the body are not different, but the same thing at different levels or frequencies of fluidity and vibration.

Fifth and perhaps the most important of all of Swedenborg's doctrines for a world still hedged about with sectarian conflict is that of the universality of the Divine Presence. Influx flows not only into a chosen people or a special sacred tradition, but "Every created thing . . . [which] is by nature recipient of God." Likewise, every religion (or morphic field if you will), in that it aligns itself with that flow of divine love and wisdom, is a suitable expression for the divine. "Swedenborg insists that the Lord is effectively present in all religions," writes George Dole of the Swedenborg School of Religion, "with the result that the good of all religions are saved. He speaks far more affirmatively, in fact, about gentiles than about Christians. For him, a God who did not provide at least the means of salvation to everyone must be unloving, unwise, or ineffective."[8] This is another idea that, if seriously shared by humanity, offers to transform the world into a semblance of heaven.

Lastly, the natural world, for Swedenborg, is the outermost manifestation of Creation. Nature itself is filled with spiritual presence. To fail to attend to its inexhaustible lessons, let alone pollute and mis-

---

7 Emanuel Swedenborg. *The Spiritual Diary*, paragraph no. 242.

8 George Dole. "Key Concepts." In *Emanuel Swedenborg: A Continuing Vision*. Edited by Robin Larsen et al. New York: Swedenborg Foundation, 1988. p. 509. Dole is referring to Swedenborg's work *Divine Providence*.

treat it, is a crime against the Divine Order. Ecology is thus implicit not only to our survival, but to our spiritual growth and education. Every living thing is potentially related to every other, because all come from the same source (Sanskrit: *Tat tvam asi*: "Thou art that"). We must learn to live in a bio-spiritual symbiosis with the natural world.

It would be possible to continue almost indefinitely this recitation of the world-transforming ideas present in Swedenborg (that are also ideas that permeate the morphic field of our time), but perhaps this sample we have given will suffice.

WHICHEVER PERSPECTIVE we take of Swedenborg, amanuensis of the divine or genius of the humanistic (or both, if our view is sufficiently ambiguous and paradoxical), our thesis is that he announced a new movement in Western civilization that not only offered a remedy for its pathological or lopsided religious view, but one that has effected a change in the very morphic field of Western civilization, the effects of which are still reverberating—and will continue to do so in the new millennium. For a documentation of the already accomplished dimensions of this transformation, I refer the reader to *Emanuel Swedenborg: A Continuing Vision,* in which respected scholars trace the historical influence of Swedenborg into science, the arts, music, healing, political and social movements such as emancipation, suffrage, and utopian communities.

You have probably heard a similar recital from many enthusiastic Swedenborgians. The thrust of the current thesis is, however, not just to trace Swedenborg's *influence* in a linear, causal way, but to treat Swedenborg himself as a necessary catalyst, himself a symbol, of the morphic or holistic movement of forces of our time. After all, if time and space are the relative categories spoken of by the New Physics, Swedenborg appeared not only because of the forces that anteceded him and of which he represented a culmination, but because we of the twentieth century, in a teleological sense, *needed him* to have been there, to pave the way for the powerful spiritual and cultural movements in the world of today. In Jungian–Gnostic terms, he embodied the *Anthropos,* the quintessential human of our time: Aquarius, the water-bearer, pouring out an inexhaustible stream of truths to a spiritually thirsty generation and announcing the signatory themes of a new millennium.

STEPHEN AND ROBIN LARSEN are co-directors of the Center for Symbolic Studies in New Paltz, New York, and co-authors of *A Fire in the Mind: The Life of Joseph Campbell.* Robin is editor of *Emanuel Swedenborg: A Continuing Vision,* and Stephen is author of *The Shaman's Doorway* and *The Mystic Imagination.* Stephen was on the board of directors for the Swedenborg Foundation for fourteen years.

ROBERT BLY

He Wanted to Live His Life Over

"What? You want to live your life over again?"
"Well, I suppose, yes . . . That time in Grand Rapids . . .
My life—as I lived it—was a series of shynesses."

"Being bolder—what good would that do?"
"I'd open my door again. I've felt abashed,
You see. Now I'd go out and say, 'All right,

I'll go with you to Alaska.' Just opening the door
From inside would have altered me—a little."
"I'm too shy . . ." "And so, a bolder life

Is what you want?" He says, "We could begin now.
Just walk with me—down to the river.
I'll pretend this boat is my life . . . I'll climb in."

ROBERT BLY is a poet, storyteller, translator, and worldwide lecturer. His poetry has won many honors, including the National Book Award.

RALPH E. PRAY

An American on Mt. Fuji

Katsushika Hokusai (1760–1849). *Fuji Above the Lightning.* From the series "Thirty-six Views of Fuji." Woodblock print, 14¾×10 inches. New York: The Metropolitan Museum of Art. Bequest of Henry L. Phillips, 1939 (JP 2961).

AS A TEMPORARY RESIDENT OF JAPAN from New Mexico, anxious to see as much of the country as possible, I left Yokohama to climb Mt. Fuji in late July. For the Japanese, to climb to the peak is the spiritually cleansing pilgrimage of a lifetime. Between 50,000 and 100,000 people of all ages walk up the mountain each summer season. I believed I was making the trip to see and photograph the surrounding view, and carried a camera on my journey.

The train leaving Yokohama dropped me off at Fujinomiya, a town at the base of Mt. Fuji. Not ten feet from the train car exit I was approached by an obviously friendly Japanese man about my age.

"I speak English," he smiled.

"I need help and my Japanese is very poor," I replied.

"Do you climb Fuji today?" he asked.

"Yes," I answered. "I have two days to visit your famous mountain, and to climb to the top."

"Where are your friends?" he asked.

"I am alone," I answered, "and travel very fast."

As we conversed further it became apparent that his English was far better than my Japanese, and he understood even more than he could say. He was Ishikawa, a school teacher.

"You need a walking stick," he explained. "You can buy one in the shop," he said, as he pointed down the street.

The six-foot sticks of freshly carved wood were sturdy, and fit the hand snugly. He picked one out, for which the shopkeeper received 120 yen.

"Come with me. You can start over there." He pointed to a group of white-clad people lining up near a wide path, which was the starting point to climb Mt. Fuji.

"Why do the people wear white?" I asked.

"It is a tradition on Fuji," he answered, "A ceremony."

There is a Japanese saying about Mt. Fuji, which translates into "A wise person climbs to the top of Fujiyama." Viewed from my offices and laboratory in far-off Yokohama, the majestic Fuji appeared to be a pinnacle from which Japan could be briefly held in the eye.

Now, at the base of the mountain, the only American in that part of Japan, on the only mountain in sight, my climb began. Mt. Fuji is not really a "climb." It is just a long, long zig-zag walk on a firmly packed volcanic cinder path.

Entire, well-provisioned families; large groups of chattering children dressed in neat uniforms; young couples with glances skittering over each other; solitary, frowning old men; and attractive women in unusual all-white kimonos, with silk parasols; were all walking single file at the same pace up the winding trail. For several hours during the splendid summer afternoon, I passed hundreds of people of all ages, talking in both English and Japanese. All of the teachers walking with children spoke a little English, and appeared anxious to try it out. They particularly enjoyed answering questions addressed to them in English, and made no attempt to teach Japanese words.

Every thirty minutes or so the trail widened, and a small rock house perched on the edge, with family members hovering over a black stove. A teapot warmed on the grill. Each time I approached a teahouse, an old woman would come forward and bow repeatedly, calling in a sing-song invitation to come to the stove. A small cup of green tea was offered and, as one reached for the cup with one hand, the walking stick was gently disengaged from the other. A branding iron was then removed from the charcoal pit and the hot end applied to the stick. One of the teachers explained that each teahouse has its own brand, and as the mountain is ascended the stick becomes covered by the distinctive burn marks.

Late into the day, and halfway up the 12,388-foot mountain, many of the children dressed in school uniforms crossed from the path going up to the path going down. I then found a large teahouse in which sleep was possible for a few hours.

Grey dawn arrived early, and the trek continued up the side of the Divine Mountain. At about 10,000 feet of elevation the physical challenge began, and the hurried pace required a strong concentration on achieving the pinnacle.

Then, as the sun rose over the Pacific, all of the blues and greens rippled brightly out of the grayness below. Everything beautiful was now separate and far away from the mountain. From high on the side of the massive declivity, Fujiyama did not seem to run like a silken thread through the everyday lives of eighty million Japanese people.

At the top of the sacred Fuji-san is a small post office, a small shrine, and a teahouse. A friendly Shinto priest greeted each new arrival in front of the shrine, and pinned a red-colored ribbon on their white clothing.

The objective of my climb, to see and photograph the vast expanse of land and sea below me, was forgotten. The camera, and the eyes, were useless. After viewing Fuji from afar in all its daily earth–sky transformations, and finally arriving at its peak, I began to understand the true reason for the stepwise ascension. One does not purposefully view Japan from Fuji. What is best perceived from the place where the earth meets the heavens occurs with the eyes closed.

Could it be that acquiring spiritual awareness inevitably entails being limited and defined, while only tending toward or seeking out such awareness allows one to remain unbound, pursuing always the infinite? And may not the search for awareness be therefore higher than its possession?

I like the suggestion, the incipienticity, the near commencement of spiritual awareness, the brief rain on the hot desert floor, and much prefer it to actual possession which, in truth, we may never have. Thus the suggestion of spiritual awareness is pictured in the mind on a higher plane than its possession. And climbing to the top of the mountain is to go to this suggestion. It is really a journey into the heart, with a singular, strange, and unforgettable arrival at the great friend in the sky.

RALPH E. PRAY has traveled widely in his work in mine property evaluations and holds degrees from the School of Mines, University of Alaska (B.S.), and the Colorado School of Mines (D.SC.). He is headquartered at his Mineral Research Laboratory near Los Angeles, and is leaving shortly for central Siberia to build a gold refinery for private Russian industry. Ralph has been writing for publication for thirty-seven years.